P9-BBV-671

Dogs to the Rescue

Dogs to the Rescue

M.R. WELLS

HARVEST HOUSE PUBLISHERS
EUGENE, OREGON

Unless otherwise indicated, all Scripture quotations are from The Holy Bible, New International Version®, NIV®. Copyright © 1973, 1978, 1984, 2011 by Biblica, Inc.™ Used by permission. All rights reserved worldwide.

Verses marked MSG are from The Message. Copyright © by Eugene H. Peterson 1993, 1994, 1995, 1996, 2000, 2001, 2002. Used by permission of NavPress Publishing Group.

Verses marked NLT are from the Holy Bible, New Living Translation, copyright © 1996, 2004, 2007 by Tyndale House Foundation. Used by permission of Tyndale House Publishers, Inc., Carol Stream, Illinois 60188. All rights reserved.

Verses marked NASB are from the New American Standard Bible®, © 1960, 1962, 1963, 1968, 1971, 1972, 1973, 1975, 1977, 1995 by The Lockman Foundation. Used by permission. (www.Lockman.org)

Verses marked CEV are from the Contemporary English Version © 1991, 1992, 1995 by American Bible Society. Used with permission.

Cover design by Left Coast Design, Portland, Oregon

Cover photo © bluecrayola / Shutterstock

Published in association with the literary agency of Mark Sweeney & Associates, Bonita Springs, FL 34135.

The information shared by the author is from her personal experience and the personal experience of others. It should not be considered professional advice. Readers should consult their own health care and dog care professionals regarding issues related to their own health and safety and the health, safety, grooming, and training of their pets.

All the incidents described in this book are true. Where individuals may be identifiable, they have granted the author and the publisher the right to use their names, stories, and facts of their lives, including composite or altered representations. In all other cases, names, circumstances, descriptions, and details have been changed to render individuals unidentifiable.

DOGS TO THE RESCUE
Copyright © 2014 by M.R. Wells
Published by Harvest House Publishers
Eugene, Oregon 97402
www.harvesthousepublishers.com

Library of Congress Cataloging-in-Publication Data
Wells, M.R. (Marion R.), 1948-
Dogs to the rescue / M.R. Wells.
    pages cm
ISBN 978-0-7369-4956-9 (pbk.)
ISBN 978-0-7369-4957-6 (eBook)
1. Dogs—Religious aspects—Christianity. 2. Dog owners—Prayers and devotions. I. Title.
BV4596.A54W445 2014
242—dc23
                                                        2013013797

All rights reserved. No part of this publication may be reproduced, stored in a retrieval system, or transmitted in any form or by any means—electronic, mechanical, digital, photocopy, recording, or any other—except for brief quotations in printed reviews, without the prior permission of the publisher.

Printed in the United States of America

14 15 16 17 18 19 20 21 22 23 / VP-JH / 10 9 8 7 6 5 4 3 2 1

To all my old and new friends, both two-footed and four-footed,
who provided inspiration and stories for these pages,
and to my loving Lord, who wove it all together—
this book's for you!

A Paw Up

I should have known that I couldn't write a book about "Dogs to the Rescue" without being rescued myself. It was a rescue of the heart. I was renewed by being reminded afresh of the hugely sacrificial love of so many dogs and humans, and of our Savior God. I am unspeakably grateful to every person and dog in these pages, and to my incredible team at Harvest House Publishers. You have given me a "paw up" in more ways than you know. A special shout-out is due to my agents, Mark and Janet Sweeney, and my editor, Rod Morris, for their invaluable support. I am also deeply grateful to Dottie P. Adams, Nicole Overbey, DVM, and Pastor Jim Leonard for their review and suggestions.

Most of all, I am grateful to God. You, O Lord, are the source of all rescue and all life, and the reason for this book!

Contents

Part 1
Special Dogs for Special Needs

Part II
A Helping Paw in Trouble

Part III
Four-Foots Lifting Four-Foots

Part IV
Comfort Is a Warm Puppy

Introduction
The Dog Who "Yelled" Fire

Caleb the Korean jindo dog was already starring in two stories for this book, so I didn't expect last night's email from his human. Pamela wrote, "Too bad your book is done because tonight Caleb saved me, Zoe, Louie Belle, the chickens, and our house."

Zoe is Pamela's other dog. Louie Belle is the cat. Apparently, about midnight, Caleb begged Pamela to come outside. She finally gave in and followed him, turning on the yard light. She and her husband, Jay, who was then at work, have four chickens housed in a movable chicken run with a coop attached. Caleb circled the chickens' enclosure, and Pamela noticed that they were all crowded together by the little gate at the end of the run. This was not normal, since chickens enter their coop as soon as it is dark and won't leave it *at all* until daylight. Nor would they be bird-brained enough to expose themselves to the freezing-cold winter weather.

When she investigated, Pamela saw that the chickens' hanging heat light had somehow come loose and fallen to the ground. Jay had just reseeded the yard and covered everything with straw. Since the coop had no flooring, the heat light was lying directly on the straw-covered grass. The bulb had a cage around it, but the heat light had fallen so the bulb was touching the straw. That straw was smoking. "If it had caught fire," Pamela noted, "the flames would have spread via the straw right across the yard to our wooden deck and then quickly to the house. God bless my smart pup for telling me something was wrong. And thank God that I listened to His furry messenger."

The great irony in all of this is that Jay makes his living as a *fire captain*. He is on the job for 24 hours at a time. While he was off saving others, his own house might have gone up in smoke—but for the stellar instincts and quick action of a faithful dog.

This great story is a capsulated version of why this book was written. Dogs are a gift from God and a means of His rescue. They seem to sense things we humans don't. They are often willing to do what we can't or won't do for ourselves or each other. And in the caring, faithful, ongoing way they love and help us, they point us to God and His rescue.

I knew I would be blessed in gathering stories for this book. I didn't have a clue how much! I have been humbled and inspired, not just by the dogs in these tales but by the incredible people who team with them. I pray these stories will grab your heart too and draw you close to your dogs, your humans, and our unfathomably loving God who made us for each other and Himself!

Meet the Author's Pups
Mica, Becca, and Marley

Becca, Marley, and Mica are a trio of pint-sized "toy joys" who are dearly loved furry companions and writing buddies.

Becca is a beautiful apricot-and-white Pomeranian fox. She loves to go "trick and treating," performing for goodies. She also loves giving doggie kisses and getting belly rubs.

Marley is a gorgeous sable-and-white papillon mix. He's the resident doggie man of the house. He delights to watch over his women—canine, feline, and human. An empathetic little guy, he is right there with a comforting smooch if he senses his mom is upset.

Mica is a stunning sable-and-white poshie (Pomeranian/toy sheltie mix). She adores everyone and never met a four-foot she didn't want to play with. But her favorite partner in doggie crime is Marley. She could wrestle and chase with him all day.

Mica is the only author's pup with a story in this book—"Half Pound Savior." But not to worry—Becca and Marley have tales in the author's previous titles, so they've gotten their share of attention too.

Part I

Special Dogs for Special Needs

🐾 Juno 🐾

D-O-G Spells Miracle
God Rescues in Miraculous Ways

The most astonishing thing about miracles is that they happen.
G.K. CHESTERTON

How could a three-and-a-half-year-old boy and a Belgian Malinois dog, both under death sentences, bring each other new life? Because God answered a father's prayer, and miracles still happen!

The little boy is Lucas Hembree. When he was two and a half years old, he was diagnosed with an extremely rare ailment called Sanfilippo syndrome. Due to a genetic mutation, a vital enzyme needed by the body is either absent or present only in very low amounts. Lucas's dad, Chester, likens the enzyme to a garbage truck inside the body that breaks down and recycles cellular waste. Little or no enzyme means the waste builds up in all the wrong places. On a biological level, the body becomes like a hoarder's home where junk piles up instead of getting dumped. Over time, this has devastating effects. The largest impact is neurological, but skin, hair, joints, bones, and vital organs are also affected. Lucas has problems with his heart and also has seizures. Afflicted children get progressively worse. Average life expectancy is

10 to 15 years, and they become vegetative and unresponsive in later stages of the disease.

When Lucas's parents, Chester and Jennifer, first heard their son's diagnosis, they knew it would not be an easy journey. They told God, *We can't do this by ourselves. But we know that You will be by our side.* Since then, Chester said, God has met all their needs—including the service dog of their dreams.

The idea of a dog came up because when Lucas was three and a half, his joints were breaking down and stiffening. It was harder for the boy to move around. Chester had been in law enforcement and helped train police dogs, and he thought a properly trained service dog could help steady Lucas and give him greater mobility for a longer time.

But when Chester talked to service dog organizations, they felt Lucas was not a good candidate. They said it wouldn't work. Chester was disheartened, but not defeated. His gut still told him this was right, so he prayed, *Lord, I know if this is in Your will, You will make it happen.*

Chester started looking at rescue dogs online and found a female Belgian Malinois in a shelter two-hours' drive from their Tennessee home. This was the breed he'd helped train for police work, and he felt this kind of dog could work really well for Lucas. Little did he know the dog was on death row. When he called, they told him she would soon be put down. Why? Because she'd just been there too long.

"Don't do anything! We're on our way," Chester said.

All the Hembrees, including big sister Allee, went to check out the potential new family member. Chester took the dog to a walking area to see if she'd pull while on leash. She walked perfectly on a loose lead. Lucas was sitting off to the side in his wheelchair, and Chester let go of the leash to see how she'd react to the boy. She went right to him and sat down next to his chair. Lucas started petting her. Chester thought, *That's it!*

The Hembree family took the dog home and named her Juno. They figured they would give her a month to adjust before the training would start, but Juno had other plans—and an awesome surprise!

Just a couple of weeks after joining her new family, Juno was with them in the living room where they were watching television. Lucas was in his wheelchair, and Juno started pacing and circling the chair. Then she began to whine and nudge the child with her nose. Juno went to his mom and dad and did the same thing. She kept going back and forth between the boy and his parents. Chester grabbed a pulse oximeter to check his son's pulse and the level of oxygen in his blood. Lucas's oxygen level was 70 percent, which is in the danger zone. Then Lucas started having a seizure. Without having any training, Juno had alerted them that Lucas was in trouble.

Over the two years the Hembrees have had Juno, she has continued to alert to seizures and low oxygen levels. Juno has saved the day multiple times. Two in particular stand out to Chester.

In one instance, Chester and his family were at a local theme park, watching a show. Juno started whimpering as she does when something isn't right with Lucas. They checked the child out, but he seemed fine. Still, Chester didn't think this was a false alarm, and he advised Jennifer that they needed to keep a close watch on their son. Two hours later, when they were leaving the park, Lucas suddenly had a very bad seizure in the car and began projectile vomiting. They rushed him to the hospital. That night in the emergency room, Lucas had 14 seizures back-to-back. It turned out he was having an allergic reaction to a new medication. He was in the hospital for two weeks.

Another episode happened at a hotel. Lucas sees various specialists at Monroe Carell Jr. Children's Hospital at Vanderbilt in Nashville, Tennessee, some distance from his home. His parents try to schedule all his appointments at one time, and the family often stays in the area overnight. Part of Lucas's prescribed regimen is water therapy, and his parents were in the hotel swimming pool with him. Juno was poolside, lying by a chair, as she'd been told. Normally she wouldn't budge, but this day, she suddenly jumped up, came over to the side of the pool, and whimpered. They checked Lucas, saw he was starting to have a seizure, and got him out of the pool before the full seizure hit.

Juno has helped with mobility too. She took to her training beautifully and has served Lucas as both a walking cane and an anchor. Juno wears a special harness with a handle. Lucas holds on to the handle and Juno slows him down and steadies him. If Lucas starts to lose his balance, Juno pushes back against him to keep him from going down. Juno has also anchored the boy. Chester explained that his son doesn't realize his limitations. His instinct is to take off and run, but he would fall and get hurt if he did so. To prevent this, boy and dog are tethered together. One end of the tether strap is fastened around Lucas's waist. The other end is attached to Juno's harness. If Lucas drops the handle of the harness, Juno lies down, forcing Lucas to come to a halt.

Sadly, these days, Lucas and Juno can't walk by themselves anymore. His disease has progressed too far. His has been a rapid decline, and at age five and a half he is showing symptoms more often seen in older children. His heart and lung involvement is such that he gets out of breath in just a few steps. Now when he does any walking with Juno, a parent or nurse is always on the other side of him.

Juno not only steadies Lucas physically, she anchors him emotionally too. She is devoted to him, and her presence calms him down. This is huge because he gets agitated due to his neurological issues. Recently Juno became ill and had to spend some time at the vet, and while she was gone, the family went to the Shriner's Circus. Lucas was much harder to handle without his faithful canine best friend by his side. Which bears out the truth of a T-shirt Chester ordered for his son: "The other angels were busy so God sent me a Belgian Malinois."

Chester and his family don't know how long they will have Lucas with them. They draw strength and courage from their faith in God. They have relied on Him to provide all their needs, and He keeps doing so in amazing ways. Just recently, someone stole their emergency generator. Within a day they were offered a new one. Someone had purchased a new generator and gave the company their old one. Learning of Chester's need, the company offered it to the Hembrees for free. They said they were just passing it forward.

Lucas has a Facebook page where his family shares his journey. They believe God entrusted Lucas to them. They want his life to have a purpose and feel if their experiences can encourage others in their faith, his life will not be wasted.

Thinking of Lucas and his family and the miracles they have seen reminds me of a miracle story from the Bible. It involves an encounter between Jesus and a blind man. John 9 tells the story. In verses 1-3 we read, "As [Jesus] went along, he saw a man blind from birth. His disciples asked him, 'Rabbi, who sinned, this man or his parents, that he was born blind?' 'Neither this man nor his parents sinned,' said Jesus, 'but this happened so that the works of God might be displayed in him.'"

Jesus proceeded to spit on some dirt and make mud, which He smeared on the man's eyes. Then He told the fellow to go wash in the Pool of Siloam. The man obeyed, and his sight was restored.

Sadly, the Pharisees didn't embrace this miracle from God. Many of them weren't fans of Jesus to begin with. What's more, the healing had happened on the Sabbath. They classified it as "work" and claimed Jesus had broken the Sabbath by His actions. After some back and forth with the once-blind man, they rejected him. When Jesus heard of it, He sought the fellow out. Jesus revealed He was the Messiah, and the man believed and received his spiritual sight on top of the physical healing.

This man's story couldn't get on Facebook, though it made it into the pages of the Bible. And for the past nearly 2000 years, it has encouraged other people's faith and drawn them to the Lord. That miracle of physical and spiritual rescue has multiplied itself manifold times and has glorified God greatly.

Lucas may not have much time left in this world. But when he walks through death's doorway, he'll be healed and whole in God's presence forever. Meanwhile his story, his family's faith, and a marvelous miracle dog named Juno will be beacons pointing others to the Lord, just like the blind man did.

This salvation, which was first announced by the Lord, was confirmed to us by those who heard him. God also testified to it by signs, wonders and various miracles, and

by gifts of the Holy Spirit distributed according to his will (Hebrews 2:3-4).

Consider This:

Has God ever rescued you or someone you know in a miraculous way? What happened? How did it affect your life? How did it impact your faith in God and influence your concept of Him? Do you have a favorite miracle in the Bible that has grown your faith in the Lord?

Duke's Doggie Day Care
God's Rescue Perseveres

'Tis not enough to help the feeble up,
but to support them after.
WILLIAM SHAKESPEARE

Duke was a marvelous German shepherd who belonged to my friend Dora. He was also a natural caregiver. When Dora brought her first child home from the hospital, Duke would park himself under her son's crib and literally babysit. Later, after her daughter was added and the kids were old enough to play in the yard, Duke would watch over them there. If they got too close to the fence, he'd corral them and guide them away.

All this was fairly normal doggie-day-care stuff. But a crisis was looming that would push Duke's caregiving to a whole new level.

When her children were still small, Dora suddenly became paralyzed on the right side of her body. She had actually had a prior incident that was related but didn't realize what it was. She had vision problems shortly before her daughter's birth, but she had also bumped her head and thought that's what had caused her trouble, especially since her vision cleared up.

This was different. It was obvious something was drastically wrong.

Dora spent ten days in the hospital having tests. Doctors suspected multiple sclerosis (MS), but they weren't sure. This happened almost 40 years ago, and they didn't have all the diagnostic tools they have today. The doctors decided it would take a third episode to make a firm diagnosis. When a young resident broke the news to her, Dora didn't even realize what he was saying. She thought he was telling her she was "a mess," not that she might have MS. Eventually the diagnosis would be confirmed and Dora would learn that she had a type of MS called relapsing-remitting, where there are episodes of illness but there may be remission in between.

Dora went home and the paralysis eventually subsided. But it took time. Meanwhile the family had to cope. Duke realized his beloved Dora needed his help, and he stepped up in a wonderful way. Dora's husband, Gary, would open the downstairs sofa bed by their half bathroom so she could lie there during the day. But she could not get out of bed by herself and needed help to answer nature's call. In a marvelous role reversal, Duke taught himself to "take his human potty," freeing Gary from having to be constantly close by.

When Dora needed such assistance and Gary wasn't home, she would tell Duke, "Potty time." He would put his head on the bed and she would grab his collar. Then he would start slowly, gently backing away to pull her up. Once upright, she could get her feet over the side of the bed. From there she could grab onto various supports and make her way into and out of the bathroom.

I see a number of wonderful lessons in Duke's gentle care of his master. Duke did it all for love. He didn't think, *Now wait a minute, this isn't right! Humans take their dogs potty, not the other way around.* He didn't wonder, *Just how long am I going to have to do this? I don't want to sign up if there's no end in sight.* Duke also didn't get burned out and up and quit one day. His attitude was, *I'm there as long as she needs me.* He was so devoted to Dora that he hated to have her out of his sight. Much later, after the paralysis subsided, the family moved to a new home. On moving day, Dora put Duke in a closed room for his safety. Being separated upset him so much that he chewed the doorknob to a cone in his efforts to get out and go to her.

Dora tells me Gary has been completely devoted too. Theirs was a storybook romance and marriage. At first, it seemed the young couple had a picture-perfect life, but that picture soon changed. Dora's first pregnancy ended in a miscarriage. Their next child, their son, was born three months premature and weighed only two pounds ten ounces. They weren't sure if he would survive.

At that time, Dora knew Jesus but Gary didn't. They went to a church service together, and the pastor told a story about a young father whose son was dying. The father said he would always look forward to seeing his son again—in heaven. That night, Gary gave his heart to Christ. And their little son survived and thrived.

Dora also went into labor early with their daughter. Doctors stopped the labor several times before she finally gave birth in her eighth month. Their little girl also lived and did great.

Gary's love remained steadfast when they faced this new challenge with MS. He never flinched. Dora did. In her thirties, she had an episode of MS where she couldn't feel her left side. She decided enough was enough. She didn't want to live like this. She didn't want to put her family through it. She would simplify things for everyone.

Dora planned her suicide for six months. Once she got her affairs in order, she tried to prepare her husband. The night before she planned to do the deed, she started telling Gary not to feel guilty. He caught on to what was happening, sat straight up in bed, and told her, "If you're planning to do what I think you are, don't you dare!" She now calls this a "come to Jesus" moment. She abandoned her suicide plans, but she couldn't make the thoughts go away. She told Gary he'd better take the gun and hide it.

A few weeks later, she landed in the hospital with gallstones and had her gallbladder removed. This was major surgery back then. Afterward, she began hemorrhaging. She was hospitalized for a month, and the surgeons had to go in three more times to get the situation handled. More than once, she could feel herself start to slip away. She begged God to spare her life because she didn't want to leave her family. This made her realize she hadn't really wanted to die after all. But she easily could have gone through with the suicide if Gary's (and God's) steadfast love hadn't stopped her.

Duke's and Gary's faithful, patient, sacrificial love for Dora mirrors the incredibly steadfast, unconditional love and patience God has for us. Dogs and even humans have limited knowledge, but God knew full well what rescuing us would cost. He had to send His Son to the cross to pull us up from sin and death. And He has to deal continually with our "relapsing-remitting" spiritual numbness, paralysis, and stumbling.

Even so, God doesn't quit. He doesn't flinch. He keeps reaching out to us, to lift us. An amazing example of this is Israel's whole history, including the section recorded in the book of Judges. God had rescued the Israelites from Egypt, sustained them in the desert, and brought them safely into the Promised Land. He had given them victory over its pagan inhabitants. He had warned them, through Moses and Joshua, to keep His ways and worship Him only. If they did, they would be blessed. But if they turned to idols, curses would come.

Sadly, the Israelites didn't listen. Spiritually speaking, they became "a mess." They started worshipping pagan gods and became spiritually numb and paralyzed. Worse, they refused to recognize their true spiritual condition. But when things got bad enough—when the curses came true and they were attacked and oppressed by the pagans around them—they eventually cried out to God for help. And He never quit responding to them. He kept sending them a "Duke"—a judge to pull them up out of their troubles. For a time, they would cling to God again. But as the years passed, they would relapse into idolatry. Yet, in spite of all their failures and unfaithfulness, He remained faithful—and is faithful still!

Jesus's death paid for our sins once and for all time, if we trust in Him. That rescue never needs to be repeated. But in this fallen world, our issues and problems often don't stay fixed. We need rescue in an ongoing way. Duke and Gary understood this and kept being there for Dora because love for her compelled them. God's unsearchable, unconditional love for His children compels Him to keep being there for us too. He has promised He won't ever forsake or leave us.

He also calls us to keep being there for others in His name. Are there people in your life who need to grab onto your "collar" so you can gently and lovingly lift them up?

"Listen to me, you descendants of Jacob,
all the remnant of the people of Israel,
you whom I have upheld since your birth,
and have carried since you were born.
Even to your old age and gray hairs
I am he, I am he who will sustain you.
I have made you and I will carry you;
I will sustain you and I will rescue you."
(Isaiah 46:3-4)

CONSIDER THIS:

Have you ever needed rescue in an ongoing way? What happened? Who helped pull you up? How did this help you see God's love and faithfulness? How can you do this for others?

Nuzzle Therapy
Love Breaks Through

Love recognizes no barriers. It jumps
hurdles, leaps fences, penetrates walls to
arrive at its destination full of hope.
MAYA ANGELOU

Can a dog jump in where caring humans haven't found a way to tread? In the case of a boy named Iyal with fetal alcohol syndrome and a very special golden retriever named Chancer, the answer is a resounding yes!

Iyal's mother, Donnie, and her husband, Harvey, got married later in life. They were not able to have children of their own. They were thrilled to adopt two 14-month-old orphans from Russia—a boy and a girl, unrelated, just two days apart in age. Daughter Morasha developed typically. Son Iyal was a different story. Soon after he turned three, his behavior grew concerning. He was impulsive and explosive. He threw tantrums and flew into rages—even in the middle of the night.

The family's tension level skyrocketed as they took him from doctor to doctor. After many months and extensive testing, their already storm-tossed lives were hit by a category five hurricane of a diagnosis. Iyal had fetal alcohol syndrome (FAS), the most severe in a spectrum of effects caused by damage to an unborn child's brain and central nervous system from alcohol consumed by the mother during pregnancy.

Donnie has explained this to Iyal as "having a boo-boo on the brain." His brain is like a strainer—it sifts things but it doesn't process them normally. And when the dots don't connect, the result can be chaos. Iyal has huge mood swings. He doesn't form attachments normally. There is an ever-widening gap between his developmental age and his chronological age. At present, Iyal is an intellectual and emotional 7-year-old trapped in a 14-year-old's body.

So, what has this meant in practical terms? Before Chancer, it meant unrelenting stress. Iyal's parents lived in a constant state of high alert. They never knew what Iyal might do or when he might blow up. Donnie described it as trying to walk on a log bobbing on a wave-tossed sea. It was exhausting. Over time, it wore Donnie and Harvey down. Their marriage grew raw and brittle. Their financial and emotional reserves were drained. Instead of coming together, they were retreating into themselves. The fabric of their family was strained and stretched and frayed and threatening to pull apart.

Even so, disrupting the adoption was never an option for Donnie and Harvey. Iyal was their son, they loved him, and they would not let him go. But the pressure was enormous. Harvey is a rabbi and is used to counseling others—to being their anchor. Now he'd been swept up in his own maelstrom of suffering and despair, and it seemed there was nothing and no one to give them hope.

Enter Chancer.

It was Donnie who came up with the idea to get Iyal a service dog. She read about an assistance dog helping a child with autism. Her late mother had always loved animals, and she felt as if this was something her mother would want her to do. Harvey vehemently disagreed. He saw the dog as piling more work on top of an already unbearable mountain. He begged his well-meaning wife to forget it. He even went so far as to say she would have to choose between a dog and him. But she was drowning and this was the only hope in sight. So she made a phone call.

Donnie called 4 Paws for Ability, the nonprofit organization that had trained the "autism dog." They asked questions. As she answered, her heart sank. Surely they wouldn't approve a service dog for her son. She braced herself for the no she would get. To her amazement, she got a yes instead. After requesting and receiving incredibly detailed information about Iyal and their family, including extensive video, 4 Paws matched the boy with Chancer. With guarded optimism, Harvey caved and gave his okay.

Since service dogs must have an adult handler, Donnie and both her children drove the 500 miles to meet Chancer and participate in several days of training. Donnie and Morasha fell in love with the dog instantly. Not Iyal. He couldn't focus on the dog for long or form an attachment easily. Not to worry. Chancer took the lead in their bonding. As Donnie put it, "Chancer seemed to know Iyal was his."

That was five years ago. In the interim, Chancer has given this boy and this family a new lease on life. Chancer has done this through a unique and loving dog-boy relationship. You could say Chancer has "kissed" Iyal's brain boo-boo and made life better in ways that caring humans couldn't.

One way Chancer has done this is to interrupt Iyal's tantrums. He was taught to do this in training. If the boy is raging, Chancer will go and find him, break through Iyal's crossed arms with his head, and nuzzle and lick him all over. This soothes Iyal. Two weeks after they brought Chancer home, Iyal told his mother that the dog was his new best friend and was like a brother. "If I'm crying, he kisses me to make me feel better," Iyal said.

This is especially significant because Iyal spent the first 14 months of his life in an orphanage. He wasn't handled and cuddled like babies need to be. This in itself is known to have negative effects on brain development. Could it be that Chancer's nuzzling is somehow helping to rewire the affected neural pathways? Donnie doesn't know, but she does know that Iyal now looks for this nuzzling from his dog. She will even tell him to go find Chancer when he is getting agitated. He might resist at first, but eventually he'll do it.

There are also times when Iyal yells at Chancer to go away. But the dog was chosen carefully. Chancer has very high self-esteem, and he isn't put off. He always comes back to his boy, no matter what. He has become Iyal's anchor.

This dog-boy bond has had some unexpected side benefits. Iyal has been able to express his feelings through his dog. For example, when he thought Chancer was smiling at another child, he told his mom, "I think Chancer wants to go home with that boy. But I don't want him to. He's my dog."

Since getting Chancer, Iyal has also been able to put words together in a more sophisticated way. Donnie can't be sure why, but she has a theory. She suspects it has to do with Chancer relaxing her son. Having his stress level lowered might allow him to access different parts of his brain.

On some level, Iyal is aware that his behavior can be a problem. His mood disorder is like a switch flipping in his brain. He will melt down, then have flashes of remorse. He will cry and wail and say he's a bad boy. He's expressed fear that he'll be sent back to Russia. Donnie has tried to remove shame and blame. She has reassured Iyal that his condition is not his fault. "Things happen that make people different," she tells him.

Sadly, that truth doesn't prevent some rather painful situations. Being different has made it rough in school. "Different" doesn't always play well with other kids. Iyal can act inappropriately. His table manners aren't the best. The past couple of years, Iyal has been bullied. He gets desperate for acceptance and will do anything to make a friend. Once Donnie found some money missing and discovered that Iyal had taken it and given it to schoolmates so they would like him.

Morasha doesn't need presents in order to like her brother. If you asked her, she would be quick to point out that Iyal has "some good parts." Morasha says, "Iyal is very kind to little kids. He offers to tie their shoelaces for them. And he's very gentle with our Pop-Pop, who is now 88 years old! Of course he makes me crazy and embarrasses me all the time," she says with a grin, "but I'm pretty used to it. I know he doesn't mean it, and I try to remember this when I'm feeling really annoyed. Which is a lot."

Chancer can't help with all of Iyal's social speed bumps. He doesn't go to school with Iyal because service dogs always have to have an adult handler with them. A human aide accompanies Iyal instead. But when Iyal gets home, Chancer is waiting. He is the faithful, nonjudgmental pal Iyal can always count on.

And he can kiss the boy's social boo-boos in other ways. In the past, the family couldn't eat at a restaurant because Iyal wasn't able to sit still that long. Now they take Chancer and park him under the table. If Iyal gets restless, he can visit Chancer there. Other diners usually don't even know the dog is with the family till they get up to leave.

Donnie also thinks that the presence of a service dog in a vest sends a message when they're out in public. If Iyal melts down, people don't just automatically assume he's a brat or Donnie and Harvey are bad parents. They realize Iyal has medical issues that are being addressed. Donnie is hopeful this might also make such situations a bit less embarrassing for Morasha.

Chancer has made a huge difference in the lives of this family. He has lifted them out of hopelessness and despair. He may have saved Donnie's and Harvey's marriage. But he can't cure FAS. He hasn't fixed the underlying problem. Chancer hasn't rescued his people *from* suffering—he has rescued them *in* suffering.

Which is what God often does.

The Old Testament book of Job sheds some interesting light on the matter. As the book starts, we readers know more than Job does. We know that God considers Job His choice servant, but Satan has challenged that statement. Satan says, in effect, "Listen God, Job loves You only because You have given him lots of goodies. Take those goodies away, and it will be a different story." God gives Satan permission to test Job, but limits what He will allow. The result? All Job's children are killed and his worldly wealth demolished. Still, Job holds fast to God. But Satan won't admit he's wrong. Instead, he asks to do even greater damage. He says, in effect, "Okay, God, Job's been faithful so far. But if he loses his health, he'll abandon You for sure!" God gives Satan leave to afflict Job but *not* to kill him—and Job winds up covered head to toe with sores.

Now the emotional, social, and spiritual rubber starts to hit the road. The fabric of Job's marriage is strained and stretched. His wife urges him to curse God and die. He refuses, calling her "foolish." We don't get any deeper glimpse than that, but it's probably a safe bet that their home wasn't characterized by domestic bliss.

Next, three of Job's friends come to hang out with him—not to commiserate but to play the blame game. They figure Job's misfortune must somehow be his fault. They chastise him for his suffering and tell him to repent of sins he didn't commit. *Ouch!*

At this point, Job is feeling pretty put-upon by God. He starts to crack a bit. He believes God has dealt with him unjustly. He figures he's been a really good guy and doesn't deserve all this. God has been unfair and owes him an explanation!

You could say Job is throwing a bit of a spiritual tantrum. He is angry and confused. One last friend tries to tell him he's off center. God is God and can't be questioned. But Job won't hear it.

Enter God!

God comes to Job in his suffering and breaks through Job's crossed arms. He gives Job love—but not in the form of nuzzling. God gives tough love. He asks Job questions that remind Job of who He is. He reminds Job of what He has done and of His sovereignty. He takes Job to a whole new level in their relationship. And in response, Job does a 180-degree turnaround. He caves and tells God,

> "You asked, 'Who is this that questions my wisdom with
>   such ignorance?'
>   It is I—and I was talking about things I knew nothing
>   about,
>   things far too wonderful for me…
> I had only heard about you before,
>   but now I have seen you with my own eyes.
> I take back everything I said,
>   and I sit in dust and ashes to show my repentance."
>   (Job 42:3,5-6 NLT)

Job repented of demanding to know why. He grabbed onto God as his anchor in the midst of his pain. He bowed to God's sovereignty and wisdom, and acknowledged His goodness. God rescued Job *in* suffering through a deeper relationship with Him, and Job allowed his spiritual brokenness to be divinely kissed, regardless of what might happen next.

In Job's case, God chose to restore his health and fortune and give him more children. But—that doesn't always happen for us humans in this life. Nor do we always find out "why me?" this side of heaven. But if we cry out to the One who knows all things, He will come to us and be with us in our broken moments.

Iyal and his family were rescued *in* suffering by a relationship with a special dog. Donnie said she and her family were threads that were unraveling, and Chancer came and added a new thread, one that allowed them all to be rewoven into a better braid. The Bible tells us that we are all unraveling threads without God. He is the only sure anchor in a troubled, broken world. He may not change your circumstances, but He will change *you*, if you seek Him and receive His truth, as Job did.

> Because of the LORD's great love we are not consumed,
>   for his compassions never fail.
> They are new every morning;
>   great is your faithfulness.
> > *(Lamentations 3:22-23)*

CONSIDER THIS:

When was the last time a pet, a person, or the Lord rescued you in suffering? How did your rescuer show you love and serve as an anchor? Who in your world might need you to do this for them?

Steady as He Woofs
God Holds Us Up

When you get to your wit's end,
you'll find God lives there.
AUTHOR UNKNOWN

Kodie the dog is a vital support to his beloved master, Jay. At times, he literally helps hold Jay up. Jay has back trouble stemming from his naval service. One result is that his left leg goes numb, and this can cause him to lose his balance, especially when changing positions. When this happens, faithful Kodie braces Jay to keep him from falling.

This is not the only way Kodie steadies his human. Jay also suffers from post-traumatic stress disorder (PTSD). Kodie has provided huge emotional support and served as a calming influence that has made a sea change in Jay's life.

Jay got Kodie through a nonprofit organization called War Dogs Making It Home. This Chicago-based group matches rescue dogs with veterans suffering from either PTSD or traumatic brain injury (TBI). They continue to train the vets and their dogs twice a week for as long as the dog/human pairs are together.

Jay's health problems happened over time. He spent 17 years in the navy. At first, he was mostly out on ships. Jay is so tall that he was constantly hunching over climbing up and down ladders. This started taking a toll on his back. He was in chronic pain, but he kept doing his job…and began suffering from depression.

In the early 1990s Jay was switched to shore duty where he served as a military policeman. Men were returning from Desert Storm and some were suicidal. Jay had to deal with a lot of that and, in the course of it, developed PTSD. He didn't tell his wife, Pam, what was going on. He kept it all bottled up inside. But finally, both the physical and emotional trauma caught up with him.

Jay was honorably discharged from the navy in 2005. He and Pam had five kids by then and the youngest was still a baby. Jay had one back surgery that year and thinks he will need one or two more. Pam serves as his caregiver because he has some memory issues and still struggles with depression. But just over a year ago, Kodie, the 115-pound German shepherd, bounded into Jay's life and changed it forever.

Kodie was brought here from Germany to be a police dog, but he flunked out. Jay thinks the reason was hypersensitivity to loud noises. Kodie became a family pet, but he was more dog than his people bargained for, and he was surrendered to a shelter. Thanks to War Dogs, one family's loss became another's salvation when Kodie was matched with Jay.

Kodie steadies Jay in many senses of that word. When Kodie is working, he wears a special vest that has a handle Jay can hold on to or grab when he needs to. In addition to bracing Jay, Kodie helps his master go up and down stairs. Going up, Kodie pulls Jay. Going down, if Kodie senses Jay is moving too fast, he will slow to let Jay know.

Kodie helps his master get out more and stay safe when he does. If Jay starts getting too close to the street, Kodie pushes on his leg to nudge him away. Kodie is also there to help if Jay starts to lose his balance while walking. Kodie will brace himself against Jay's leg and stand there until Jay gets steady and cues his dog to start moving forward again.

Kodie is being trained to fetch things for his master too, like a cane or keys or the TV remote. Having a four-legged gofer to take over such tasks will save Jay's back from unnecessary strain.

In addition to providing physical support, Kodie has been his master's emotional rock. He can sense Jay's moods and has been trained to intervene. Jay recalls one particular day when he was out walking with Kodie and was talking with a customer service rep on his cell phone. He was getting upset and Kodie noticed. Kodie dropped to the ground and jerked Jay's arm. It was his way of saying, "Chill!" Jay took the hint and got off the phone. When he called back after taking a breather, he was better able to handle the conversation.

Kodie's presence forces Jay to socialize more than he might otherwise because his dog attracts attention. But if Kodie senses Jay doesn't want to interact, he will sit in front of his master to extend Jay's personal space. Jay says Kodie is actually more aware of his PTSD than he is. Jay may get agitated and not catch on to what is happening. But Kodie gets it…and looks at his master, cueing those around Jay that something isn't right.

At home, Kodie senses when Jay is getting agitated and will sit with a paw on each of Jay's knees. This prompts Jay to pet him, which is calming. If Jay has a panic attack while lying down, Kodie lays his head on his master's chest to help control and slow Jay's breathing. Kodie even rescues Jay from bad dreams. Sensing something is amiss, he wakes his master up.

When it comes to manners, you can take Kodie almost anywhere. He knows to go under the handicapped seat on the bus and to head under the table in restaurants.

Jay's kids are glad that Kodie is helping their dad reconnect with the world. Having Kodie has encouraged Jay to do more—even when his dog can't be right there with him. Jay has gotten involved in adaptive sports. He's gone skiing in a chair, and he and Pam have ridden 25 miles on specialized bikes. Pam no longer feels she has to stay home with Jay constantly. She knows Kodie is there to look after him. Recently she even went to a retreat for caregivers. Pre-Kodie, she would not have dared to be away from Jay that long.

For his part, Kodie hates being separated from Jay. When he is, he whines and barks in protest. It's as if he's saying, "No! You need me to be there if something happens!"

If the presence of a faithful but finite four-legged canine can have such an impact, how much more can God's presence and support change our lives? The apostle Paul gives us an inkling. Writing to Timothy while imprisoned in a dungeon under the emperor Nero, he speaks of how God has held him up:

> At my first defense, no one came to my support, but everyone deserted me. May it not be held against them. But the Lord stood at my side and gave me strength, so that through me the message might be fully proclaimed and all the Gentiles might hear it. And I was delivered from the lion's mouth. The Lord will rescue me from every evil attack and will bring me safely to his heavenly kingdom (2 Timothy 4:16-18).

Just as Kodie has done for Jay, God stood by Paul in his hour of need. God braced Paul and steadied him. Probably nudged by God's Word and God's love, Paul avoided anger and bitterness and forgave those who had left him in the lurch. And the Lord's presence protected Paul from spiritual PTSD. Rather than have a panic attack, he was able to proclaim the gospel. Instead of being plagued by bad dreams of martyrdom, Paul clung to God's promise of eternity with Him.

We are all candidates for spiritual post-traumatic stress disorder in this fallen world. We have all suffered pain and gone emotionally numb. But just as Kodie is there for Jay, God is there for us. He offers each of us His love and support and eternal presence—if we take Him into our life and heart, as Paul did.

The LORD is my light and my salvation—
whom shall I fear?
The LORD is the stronghold of my life—
of whom shall I be afraid?
                                    (Psalm 27:1)

CONSIDER THIS:

Who has been a main support for you in your life? How have they helped steady you and balance you out? How has God done these things for you? Who might you help in this way?

A Hearing Dog Goes to College
God's Presence Empowers

Security is not the absence of danger, but the presence of God, no matter what the danger.
AUTHOR UNKNOWN

For a spunky college student named Jenny, freedom has a face. That face belongs to her five-pound papillon dog. *Papillon* is French for butterfly, and Jenny's precious pup, Minnie Pearl, is giving her wings to soar to new independence despite a hearing impairment.

Jenny had hearing loss from birth, but it went undetected at first. Her mom and dad had loud voices and large mouths. She could hear some and lip read some and unconsciously learned to compensate. A preschool teacher was the first to suspect a problem. When her hearing loss accelerated at around age five, she got hearing aids, but they could do only so much.

Jenny didn't let her hearing problems cramp her style. Her mom encouraged a can-do attitude. She told Jenny the only thing she couldn't do was hear, and Jenny took these words to heart. Though she had an education plan tailored to her (she was dyslexic also), she stayed in normal classes. She even played high-school basketball. She and her teammates developed hand signals for plays. If a teammate had to get her attention, she would stomp her foot on the floor. Jenny would feel the vibration and know to look over.

Friends were also supportive in college, but Jenny began to think ahead. What would happen after she graduated? What if she were living on her own? Even if she had a roommate or got married, who could she turn to when that other person was away? Who would alert her to fire alarms and doorbells and, one day, perhaps her baby crying?

Jenny decided her answer to that question was…a dog!

Through a nonprofit organization, 4 Paws for Ability, she got hooked up with Pearl. It was a match made in doggie heaven. She fell in love with the little papillon, and discovered she and Pearl even shared the same birthday—November 15.

After appropriate training for both, Pearl has joined Jenny at college this year, and they share a townhouse with three other human roommates. Though Pearl is extra work, Jenny has already gained a lot more freedom and extra peace of mind.

Prior to Pearl, Jenny couldn't hear the microwave go off unless she was right in the kitchen. She couldn't hear the doorbell ring. Now, she doesn't have to worry as much. Pearl is trained to alert to a variety of sounds, and she goes to Jenny and paws at her. Jenny uses a word or hand signal to ask her dog, "Where?" Pearl then runs straight to the source of the noise. That is, unless the sound in question is a fire alarm, in which case the prearranged signal is for Pearl to hit the deck. This cues Jenny to scoop up her dog and head for an exit.

Pearl has also been trained to paw Jenny if someone is calling Jenny's name or even speaking it in conversation. Or, if Jenny is holding her, she squirms. And when she's in class with Jenny, she helps her stay plugged in socially. If Jenny's working on something and Pearl hears a noise, she'll perk up and look toward it. That cues Jenny to check and see what's going on.

Another place where Pearl helps out is in the car. Jenny can drive but must have extra mirrors. Still, pre-Pearl, she was often not aware of police cars, fire engines, and ambulances until they were close enough to see. Now Pearl alerts to sirens and provides an earlier heads-up that one of these vehicles may be approaching.

Jenny is a college senior, and her goal is to teach special needs kids. When she worked at a camp for such youngsters, the experience changed her life. She also believes that her own challenges help her get what these kids are going through.

Currently, Jenny is observing in a normal second-grade classroom. She gets to teach a few math lessons too. Pearl comes along, and not only for the ride. "She mostly just sits in a 'down' under the table, but she escorts me safely to and from the school," Jenny told me. "The kids love her! The first day we sat on the carpet and talked about service dogs—what they do and look like and the difference between them and a pet dog. We also talked about me being hearing impaired. I let them pet Pearl so they got that out of the way. They never asked to pet her again because they knew she was working—just like they do when they come to school."

Having Pearl with her has made all the difference to Jenny in facing life's challenges and embracing her future. Having God with us makes all the difference to His children. An ancient ruler named Jeroboam found that out, to his ruin. The Promised Land had split into two kingdoms, Israel and Judah. Jeroboam was reigning in Israel, and he had led the people into idolatry. Judah under King Abijah was staying true to the Lord. War broke out between them, and Israel fielded an army twice as big as Judah's fighting force.

King Abijah wasn't daunted. Maybe his foes had double the men, but he had God on his side. He stood atop a mountain and shouted a warning. Among other things, he said, "We are following the instructions of the LORD our God, but you have abandoned him. So you see, God is with us. He is our leader. His priests blow their trumpets and lead us into battle against you. O people of Israel, do not fight against the LORD, the God of your ancestors, for you will not succeed!" (2 Chronicles 13:11-12 NLT).

Abijah was right. Judah prevailed against this huge challenge because God was with them!

Having a hearing dog doesn't mean Jenny will have fewer challenges in life. But Pearl's presence may give her the confidence and tools to tackle and conquer what might otherwise have conquered her. In an infinitely greater way, God's presence did the same for Abijah—and will do so for you and me, if we put our trust in Him.

Whatever I have, wherever I am, I can make it through anything in the One who makes me who I am (Philippians 4:13 MSG).

CONSIDER THIS:

Other than God, who is the most important presence in your life right now? How does that person (or pet) help you through tough times? How does God's presence rescue you and empower you to face new challenges?

A Dog or a Wheelchair?
God's Leash Steadies Us

The dangerous falls were the ones that happened so fast you didn't have time to react.
JEANNETTE WALLS, *Half Broke Horses*

What do God and some dogs know that people often don't? They know *ahead of time* when we are about to fall. The ability to sense this danger and act to stop it has given a wonderful dog named Tribute a special place and ministry in his beloved Dora's life.

I met Dora through a mutual friend. She was diagnosed in her twenties with relapsing-remitting multiple sclerosis (MS). Over the years she's had episodes where she struggled with symptoms and times in between when the illness went into remission.

This ailment manifests in many different ways, including vision problems, numbness, paralysis, and difficulty with balance. As Dora's MS progressed, her balance issues increased. Finally, about eight and a half years ago, her balance got so bad during one MS episode that she suffered several serious falls. These falls happened with no prior warning. She told me she went down like a tree—she didn't even realize she was falling. Her doctor told her this couldn't go on and gave her a prescription for a wheelchair. But she fought the idea.

Dora and her husband, Gary, had had dogs for years. Elsewhere in this book I've told how their dog Duke helped Dora during an earlier MS episode. But they'd never thought of getting a dog trained to assist her more extensively. They were receiving a magazine about MS, and that month's issue had a photo and article about another MS patient who was being helped by a service dog. Dora read it and knew what she would do. She told Gary, "No wheelchair!" She would get their two-year-old male Labrador retriever, Tribute, trained to assist her instead.

Gary was dubious. He'd put Tribute through his early training paces as a puppy, and he would teasingly say Tribute was "the dumbest puppy" he'd ever seen. Actually, Tribute wasn't dumb, he was stubborn—but Gary didn't catch on at the time. The assistance-dog organization Dora called was dubious also. Normally they didn't like to train people's pets, but they sent a team to Dora's house to test Tribute to see if he could do the program. Tribute seemed to sense he had to perform. Though the testing team did things that would make most dogs jump or run from the room, Tribute stood his ground—and passed muster with flying colors.

There was another challenge too. Up till then, Gary had been Tribute's alpha or pack leader. Tribute now needed to transfer that allegiance to Dora. He did.

Most dogs take 18 to 24 months to complete this organization's assistance-dog training, but Tribute whipped through to graduation in a record 8 months. He aced the course and turned skeptic Gary into a believer. "I guess I was the dummy," Gary said fondly.

Tribute wears a service-dog vest and face halter when he is working. His leash is attached to the halter, which makes him aware of Dora's movements and helps him sense when she is in trouble. He steadies Dora in a variety of ways. When she is climbing stairs, he goes ahead of her, keeping the leash taut. When she is descending, he stays behind her and keeps the leash tight. Tribute has been taught to know if Dora is falling toward him or away from him and will adjust his position to steady her even before she realizes she's in trouble.

Tribute uses other tactics that he seems to have taught himself. Once when he was beside Dora and she started falling, he put his body under hers to keep her from going down. He supports her that way when she is rounding a curve on a staircase.

When Tribute's leash, vest, and halter are off, he isn't officially working, which is often the case when they are at home. Dora can usually get around fine, and if need be, will hold on to furniture, walls, doors, and counters to make her way around. But she does fall now and then. If she's alone when this happens, Tribute has been trained to bring her a phone so she can call for help. But if Gary is home, Tribute finds his master and taps him with his paw. Gary knows what this means and tells Tribute, "Take me to Dora." And Tribute does.

Tribute not only helps keep Dora safe, he widens her world. She had reached the point where she wouldn't go to the grocery store alone. With Tribute, she feels safe to venture out. Tribute's presence also frees Gary to do things on his own. Though he's devoted to Dora, and she to him, not being constantly leashed together has been calming for them both.

Tribute has also made it possible for Dora to do some volunteer work. Her involvement with Community Emergency Response Team (CERT) has been especially rewarding. Members of CERT are trained to help in crises like fires, hurricanes, and earthquakes. Part of that training involves simulations—people acting out a crisis situation as CERT members respond and implement emergency procedures in this practice setting.

Tribute always goes to CERT classes and activities with Dora. He is a member too and has his very own CERT vest. He delights to greet everyone. But in this and other situations, he will not leave Dora's side unless she gives him permission to go visit.

Tribute also won't let Dora overexert herself. She recalls one particular trip to a department store. She had a lot to get done, but at a certain point, Tribute sensed she might literally "shop till she dropped." He lay down on the floor and refused to budge. She had to call Gary to come get her.

Dora told me Tribute seems to know when something is wrong with her. One evening he started leaning into her abdominal area. Earlier that night she'd had a strange sensation and had told her husband about it "just in case something goes wrong." Later she awoke in horrific pain. Testing indicated a mass in one kidney. At first, doctors weren't sure if it was cancer or a mass of blood (infarction). Thankfully it began to go away and doctors now feel cancer was not the culprit.

Tribute reaches out to others who are hurting too—like the three-year-old they encountered while keeping a medical appointment. The little girl was in a wheelchair, and Tribute went to her and they started loving on each other. "It was such a healing moment," Dora recalled. "They were communicating on such a perfect level." When it came time to see the doctor, he told Dora she hadn't really needed the appointment at all and apologized for his staff's mistake in making it. "This appointment was no mistake," Dora told him. "Tribute and I were meant to be here for that little girl."

One additional area where Tribute rescues Dora is emotional and social. Dora explained that in the past, when she was out in public and became unsteady, she feared people would draw the wrong conclusions. She worried they might think she was tipsy or high on drugs. She sensed that people were put off and hanging back from her, and she felt terribly embarrassed. Having Tribute with her has changed that. His presence in his service-dog vest makes it clear that she has medical issues. And because people are drawn to him, they focus less on her.

MS is an unpredictable illness, and Dora isn't sure what her future holds. Just in the last two months she can't feel her feet. Tribute's future as a service dog is uncertain also. He's getting older and has some health issues. Dora realizes that before too long, she must choose a new puppy and have it trained so Tribute can pass the baton. But though what lies ahead here on earth is somewhat unpredictable, Dora knows what her *eternal* future will be. She will spend it in God's presence in a new resurrection body that is healthy and whole. And she believes her afflictions in this life have opened doors to tell others about His goodness and rescue.

I could draw a number of parallels between Tribute's rescue and God's, but one in particular stands out. It is how Tribute senses Dora might fall before she does. To me, this is a parable of how God knows we are in danger of falling in a spiritual sense. The Bible's pages are filled with examples, but I was struck by the story of Cain. Adam and Eve gave birth to him and his brother Abel. At a certain point, they both made offerings to God. Cain offered fruits of the soil and Abel offered fat portions from the firstborn of his flocks. God accepted Abel's offering but not Cain's, and this threw Cain into a murderous rage.

God knew that Cain was about to fall, and He tried to steady Cain by giving him a warning. In Genesis 4:6-7, God said, "Why are you angry? Why is your face downcast? If you do what is right, will you not be accepted? But if you do not do what is right, sin is crouching at your door; it desires to have you, but you must rule over it."

Cain didn't let God steady him. He dropped the leash by ignoring the warning and killed his brother. And because of it, he came under a curse. He was sentenced to be a wanderer. But God showed mercy and rescued Cain from human wrath by putting a protective mark on his forehead.

Dora knows Tribute is God's gift to her. Jesus is God's gift to all of us. He died to pay for all the ways we would ever fall. If we give our hearts to Him and hold fast to Him daily, He will steady us, just as Tribute does Dora.

> The LORD makes firm the steps
> of the one who delights in him;
> though he may stumble, he will not fall,
> for the LORD upholds him with his hand.
>   (Psalm 37:23-24)

CONSIDER THIS:

When did the Lord last keep you from falling? How did He steady you? What did you learn about yourself, and Him? How might He want to use you to come under and support someone else?

Sno Warning
Heed God's Heads-Up

Better three hours too soon than a minute too late.
WILLIAM SHAKESPEARE

S noball is a beautiful golden retriever who can predict the future. Okay, that's not exactly true. What this dog does is alert to seizures before they happen, which is vitally important to her person, a teen named Henna.

Henna has traumatic brain injury from abuse she suffered as a baby. At one point she was clinically dead, but the doctors managed to revive her. She had surgery and spent a month in a coma afterward. When she woke up and improved enough to be released, the two-and-a-half-year-old was placed in therapeutic foster care. Her foster parents, Jan and Chris, wound up adopting her.

Sadly, little Henna had ongoing neurological fallout. She began having seizures. Things got worse, not better, over the years. By the time she was middle-school age, she was having up to 100 seizures a day, many of them drop seizures, meaning she could fall and hurt herself. Jan thought her daughter could be greatly helped by the right assistance dog. If Henna had a dog that could alert to seizures before they happened, the people around her could take measures to help keep her safe.

Henna's first seizure-alert dog was a Labradoodle named Leo. He was big and strong enough that he could help support her weight, but he alerted to Henna's seizures only *after* the fact. If he saw his young charge begin to shake or stumble or fall, he'd bark nonstop and butt up against her to balance her. Most of the time, he kept her from falling, but Jan thought prior warning would be better still. She went back to 4 Paws for Ability, the nonprofit organization that had matched them with Leo and trained him, and they came up with a new doggie option—Sno. Jan went with Henna to train with Sno and bring the golden retriever home, and they kept Leo as a pet.

Sno will alert to an upcoming seizure by going to Henna and licking her mouth and nose profusely. Sno will also bark a warning, and she becomes more agitated when Henna's seizure activity is higher. It's like having an extra parent around to keep watch over Henna and warn of trouble before it happens.

And, like a parent, Sno does far more than help keep Henna safe. Dog and teen have formed a very special bond, one that was cemented the week after Jan and Henna brought Sno home. Henna went into the hospital for surgery. Other measures to control her seizures hadn't worked, so doctors tried a more drastic approach—separating the two hemispheres of her brain. Sno stayed in the hospital for nine days and hung out on Henna's bed. The dog alerted to seizures and also comforted Henna by laying her doggie head in Henna's lap.

As of this writing, Henna is still healing from her surgery. Only time will tell how much difference it will make. Meanwhile she is back in school. Age-wise she is now a high-school freshman, but she is more on a preschool or kindergarten level in emotional development and learning. She is in a special class with other students who have moderate intellectual disabilities. Henna has an aide assigned to her, and Sno comes to class as well. Sweet-tempered Sno has already worked her doggie magic on one of Henna's classmates who was fearful of pups. This youngster now wants to pet Sno rather than shrink away.

Henna's school won't let her aide be responsible for Sno, and someone other than Henna has to do that. So Jan has been going to high school with her daughter. She feels the measure of safety Sno adds is well worth it. And Sno's presence may also help reduce the frequency of seizures by keeping Henna calmer.

Thinking about how Sno and Leo have rescued Henna calls to mind how God seeks to rescue us. The Bible says that due to the Fall, we are all born spiritually dead. But we are revived to eternal life if we put our faith in the Messiah, Jesus, for forgiveness of our sins. Still, we have ongoing fallout from our old nature to deal with, and this can trigger spiritual drop seizures. God alerts us to our danger in various ways: through His Word, His Spirit, and godly believers, but also through other things around us, even *animals*.

In the book of Numbers, God used a donkey to warn a prophet named Balaam. Balaam may not have had a saving knowledge of God, but he should have known better than to flirt with the king of Moab's repeat request to come and curse the Israelites who were camping in Moabite territory. God had already told Balaam once not to do it and that this was a blessed people. But when new emissaries came with new inducements, Balaam seemed to hope that God might change His mind. God let Balaam set out on the journey, but He was not pleased.

Balaam's donkey wasn't pleased either. She just wouldn't stay on the road. First she veered off into a ditch. Then she veered into a fence. Finally, she just stopped in her tracks and sat down. Each time, Balaam beat the donkey, but it didn't change her mind. Finally, God stepped in and gave the donkey speech. Numbers 22:30-33 (MSG) tells what happened next:

> The donkey said to Balaam, "Am I not your trusty donkey on whom you've ridden for years right up until now? Have I ever done anything like this to you before? Have I?"
>
> He said, "No."
>
> Then GOD helped Balaam see what was going on: He saw GOD's angel blocking the way, brandishing a sword. Balaam fell to the ground, his face in the dirt.
>
> GOD's angel said to him: "Why have you beaten your poor donkey these three times? I have come here to block your

way because you're getting way ahead of yourself. The donkey saw me and turned away from me these three times. If she hadn't, I would have killed you by this time, but not the donkey. I would have let her off."

Balaam's donkey warned of danger that hadn't happened yet. In that way, she functioned like Sno the golden retriever. A certain biblical rooster acted more like Leo the Labradoodle, flagging a spiritual drop seizure after the fact.

Jesus was about to be arrested and crucified, and He warned the disciples that they would abandon Him. Simon Peter said, no way! Even if everyone else deserted Christ, he wouldn't. Jesus responded, "Today, this very night in fact, before the rooster crows twice, you will deny me three times" (Mark 14:30 MSG).

Peter did just what Jesus predicted. He didn't even realize it at first, but then the rooster crowed right on schedule. And though Peter was shaking and stumbling, he didn't quite hit bottom. He saw his sin and wept in remorse. And later, Jesus reinstated Peter and he played a key role in the early church and died a martyr's death.

Henna's parents love the Lord. They know Sno is part of His provision to keep their daughter safe, and they watch for their dog's alerts and heed them. God our Father loves us too and wants to keep us from falling. He sends "donkeys" to turn us aside, and if we don't respond, He sends "roosters" to keep us from crashing completely. He desires that we repent, like Peter did. And when we do, He is waiting to welcome us into His arms.

"Simon, Simon, Satan has asked to sift all of you as wheat. But I have prayed for you, Simon, that your faith may not fail. And when you have turned back, strengthen your brothers" (Luke 22:31-32).

CONSIDER THIS:

When was the last time God sent you a "Sno warning" of an impending spiritual drop seizure? Did you heed it? What was the result? Has He ever sent you a "Leo" to brace you when you were spiritually stumbling? How did you respond?

Her Dog Is Her Eyes
God Watches Out for Us

There is none so blind as they that won't see.
Jonathan Swift

Two strikes, you're out? That's what Judy feared—at least in the short term. She had waited many months and flown 1500 miles to the Seeing Eye training facility to meet her guide dog. The one they'd thought would be a good match had shown aggression to a trainer and flunked out. A second pooch proved too much for this first-time dog owner to handle. The 26-day training class was already half over, and Judy figured she'd be going home empty-leashed. She didn't see how another doggie match was possible in the time remaining.

Thankfully, God sees what we don't.

In this case, what God saw was a beautiful black Labrador retriever named Velda. She wasn't even supposed to be available yet. She was being groomed for the class after Judy's, but God opened the right people's eyes to this dog maybe being the one. Judy and Velda were introduced. *Home run!*

That was six years ago. In the interim, Velda's eyes have widened Judy's world. She sees light and big shadows but not much else. When she was born, incubators were new. Some babies wound up with damaged vision from oxygen levels that went too high. Judy was one of them.

Pre-dog, Judy had navigated with a cane. She thought she preferred it. Hey, a cane didn't need to be fed or go potty. But a cane had its limits too. There were hazards it could not detect, such as electric cars too quiet for Judy to hear.

Now Judy has Velda's eyes to watch for danger. Velda takes her to a corner and stops. If the dog sees traffic coming she won't budge, even if Judy orders her forward.

Velda looks out for her person in other ways too. One day she refused to proceed down the street, and Judy realized something was up and adjusted her commands. Velda led her around the obstacle. Judy later learned the sidewalk was being repaired and Velda had kept her from stepping into a construction site.

Velda also loves taking Judy shopping in big stores. Judy brings a companion along to help. The companion walks in front, pushing a cart, and Velda follows with Judy in tow.

Velda does great in airports too, and Judy finds flying much less daunting with her dog by her side. Currently she has a job that requires some distance travel. Shortly after signing on, she was at a busy airport, catching a plane. A friend was with her and said, "Boy, your dog really took you through that crowd."

"What crowd?" Judy said. She hadn't even realized there was one.

Crowd or not, Judy's less likely to bump into someone with a dog than a cane. Nor are Velda's navigational skills limited to obstacle avoidance. Velda understands a number of words. If Judy's in a public restroom, she can tell Velda, "Hup to the stall," and her dog will take her to an empty one. She can then say, "Hup to the sink," and Velda will guide her to a sink so she can wash up. Other words Velda knows include *sidewalk*, *railing*, *steps*, *dumpster*, *elevator*, and *counter*.

If Judy is outdoors and wants to go in, she need only tell Velda, "Inside." Velda will guide Judy to the door and position herself so that if Judy lifts her hand over her dog's head, it will touch the handle.

Velda's skills are a huge help when Judy is staying in a new place. She asks someone to orient both her and her dog. They learn together, and once they have, they can work as a team to navigate the new surroundings. This saves Judy from having to bother people at inconvenient times. Once she was staying at her nephew's home and needed to find the bathroom in the middle of the night. Velda helped her and Judy didn't have to wake anyone up.

Judy adores Velda and feels this dog is a wonderful fit for her. She gives big kudos to the Seeing Eye organization. Their thorough application process, careful selection, and extensive training, including in her home and neighborhood, have made all the difference. But Judy also loves the Lord, and she can see His hand in it all, especially her and Velda's initial pairing. "He made a way where there seemed no way," she told me.

Velda fits beautifully into Judy's lifestyle. They both love people, and Velda is laid back and obedient and almost never barks. Judy even takes her dog to church. And when she and her family lead praise and worship, Velda guides her up on stage and then lies quietly beside her until the singing is over.

Thinking about how Velda guides Judy reminds me that we need God to be our Seeing-Eye Master. The Bible tells us that sin clouds our vision from birth. Even when our sins are forgiven by grace through faith in Jesus and we are born into God's family, our sight still isn't what it will be one day. The apostle Paul put it this way in 1 Corinthians 13:12: "For now we see only a reflection as in a mirror; then we shall see face to face. Now I know in part; then I shall know fully, even as I am fully known."

God sees truth. He sees the future. Graciously, He puts His Spirit within His children to guide us. In John 16:13 Jesus tells His disciples that the Spirit "will guide you into all the truth."

Paul relied on the Spirit's leading to fulfill his calling as an apostle to the Gentiles. Acts 16:6-10 is a powerful example. Paul tried to go and preach the gospel in both the province of Asia and Bithynia, but the Spirit blocked his way. Then, through a vision, God sent him to Macedonia instead.

Velda guides Judy physically, but spiritually, God does. She knows the "cane" of human wisdom can do only so much. She has chosen to let her Seeing-Eye Master lead her into His truth and direct her steps. What choice will you make?

"I will lead the blind by ways they have not known,
    along unfamiliar paths I will guide them;
I will turn the darkness into light before them
    and make the rough places smooth.
These are the things I will do;
    I will not forsake them."

                                          (Isaiah 42:16)

CONSIDER THIS:

Have you ever regretted depending on the "cane" of human wisdom, instead of following your Seeing-Eye Master? How did you stumble? What did you learn? Has God ever guided you around a hazard? What happened? What were you saved from?

The Titus Connection
God Meets Us Where We Are

*You can't stay in your corner of the Forest waiting for
others to come to you.
You have to go to them sometimes.*
A.A. MILNE, *Winnie The Pooh*

Titus the dog wasn't playing by the book. He was flying by the seat of
his furry hind end. But the empathetic golden retriever was a seasoned
therapy dog. His loving owner and handler, Kris, had extensive training too, and she chose to hold back for a moment, watch carefully, and
see what would happen.

The pair were working with some special needs kids at a respite facility called Jill's House. Its purpose is to give families a much-needed
break. Its expert staff will care for these youngsters for a day or a weekend while their loved ones rest and recharge.

On this day, Titus had gone over to a child and laid his head in her
lap. They had become odd friends. She was autistic and nonverbal. She
couldn't seem to pet Titus, but would bop him on the head instead.
Still, Titus wanted to reach out. He seemed to sense she didn't mean to
hurt him but was trying to connect in the only way she knew.

Typically, if the girl bopped Titus, Kris would gently pull the dog
away. But this time, Titus wouldn't *stay* pulled away. He kept returning

to the girl, and Kris chose to let them interact very briefly as she stayed tuned to her dog's body language. Then she stepped in with a ball in her hand.

"You and Titus are doing so well, would you like to reward him?" she asked. "Titus likes it when you throw a ball."

The child threw a ball for Titus, for the very first time!

This girl progressed to giving Titus her very own brand of hug. Kris would put Titus on the floor on his side. The girl would lift one of his front legs, drape it over her neck, and bury her face in the dog's furry chest. This was a child who wouldn't stay still under normal circumstances, but she would remain in her hug with Titus for close to four minutes.

That little girl never did learn how to make a petting motion, but she'd taken some baby steps forward in connecting with others. And Titus played a significant part. He sensed the heart beneath her behavior and met her where she was, and it made a real difference.

Meeting others where they are also has to do with patience and timing. Kris's experience with another autistic child brought this lesson home in Technicolor. This little boy was involved in the Breakaway Program at McLean Bible Church, a respite-care day program offered two Saturdays a month. The child would go where he was told, but would never interact with anyone. Kris tried to get him to throw a ball for Titus too. Kris would toss the ball out in front of Titus, and he would snap it up in midair. It never got the boy's attention.

Two years passed. Kris went to a seminar, and what she learned alerted her that she might not have been patient enough with this boy. She learned that response times vary for such youngsters and could take at least ten minutes or more.

On the boy's next visit, Kris once again tried to coax him to throw a ball for Titus. Once again, nothing happened. But this time, Kris just waited. Titus stood waiting also, doggie eyes on the prize. Minutes ticked away. Titus sat. Then he lay down, gaze fixed on the ball all the while. The clock kept ticking. When it was nearly the ten-minute mark, suddenly, the boy took the ball and threw it for Titus four times in a row. Then he walked away.

Kris sat and wept. She felt she'd taken her eyes off the ball herself by being on her own timing instead of God's. This boy might have interacted sooner if only she'd had more patience. That experience taught her that God's rescue isn't on our timetable. If we don't get on His, we may miss the gift.

As Titus instinctively knew and as Kris learned, outreach has many facets. Not everyone can come to us, but if we go to them by suspending our agenda and preconceptions and looking at the heart, not the outside, wonderful things may happen.

Jesus of Nazareth, our Messiah, lived this truth when He walked on this planet. One particularly powerful example involves one of His chosen twelve, a disciple named Thomas, nowadays also known as "doubting Thomas."

Jesus had been crucified and had risen from the dead. He had appeared to His disciples, let them see His side and hands, and given them the Holy Spirit. But Thomas wasn't there when all this happened. When the others shared the great news, he didn't exactly embrace it. "But he said to them, 'Unless I see the nail marks in his hands and put my finger where the nails were, and put my hand into his side, I will not believe'" (John 20:25).

Jesus could have pulled away. He could have said, "Forget this guy. I've spent three and a half years showing him who I am. He should realize it on his own, and if not, he should certainly believe his friends. So if he won't, too bad! Time's up."

Jesus did nothing of the kind. He met Thomas where he was. John 20:26-28 reveals,

> A week later his disciples were in the house again, and Thomas was with them. Though the doors were locked, Jesus came and stood among them and said, "Peace be with you!" Then he said to Thomas, "Put your finger here; see my hands. Reach out your hand and put it into my side. Stop doubting and believe."
>
> Thomas said to him, "My Lord and my God!"

God wants to meet us where we are, and He wants us to do this for others, because He loves each of us so much. We may not all have the instincts of Titus or be all-knowing like Jesus, but we have God's Spirit if we belong to Him. If we ask, He will give us the insight and timing we need to reach out in His name and not miss the gift.

"For the Son of Man came to seek and to save the lost" (Luke 19:10).

CONSIDER THIS:

When was the last time you needed God to meet you where you were? What were you struggling with? How did He connect with you? What impact did it have on your life? When was the last time you met someone else where they were? How were you blessed?

Doggie Ears to Hear

God Helps Us Hear Him

*Blindness separates us from things, but deaf-
ness separates us from people.*
HELEN KELLER

Cookie Monster is a beautiful English setter/spaniel mix who serves as Andri's extra set of ears. She is a trained hearing dog. Cookie not only rescues Andri from everyday mishaps small and large, she eases social situations and chases Andri's loneliness away with her loving, accepting companionship.

Andri's hearing loss has been progressive. She heard well enough as a child that her speech sounds normal. But her hearing deteriorated with time. She has been hard of hearing for years, but her loss has worsened markedly in the last half decade and continues to do so. She is now legally deaf.

Andri explained that hearing aids can help only so much. It's not like putting on a pair of glasses; it's more like using a cane. You still have a limp. The aids work only with whatever hearing a person has left. With her hearing worsening, Andri decided what she needed was an extra set of *good* ears—doggie ears—to pick up what she missed and alert her.

Andri contacted Texas Hearing and Service Dogs in hopes of getting a dog from them. They adopt and train rescue dogs and pair them with people. As a part of the application process, Andri had to write an essay. "This journey into deafness is intimidating," she said in the piece. "I remember the ease with which I used to do tasks that are some days frustratingly annoying." She spoke of how cashiers would get irritated at her look of confusion, not realizing she had a hearing impairment. And how sales clerks would think her rude when she ignored their greeting. And how she'd been startled by a stranger who showed up suddenly in her apartment. It turned out he was a handyman. He'd come to make requested repairs, knocked repeatedly to no avail, and finally let himself in, shocking Andri in the process.

Andri wrote about how a hearing dog would make her feel safer and would never feel inconvenienced, but enjoy helping her. And if the pup was a little extra work, it was a small price to pay for what that extra set of doggie ears would add to her life.

Andri was green-lighted to get a dog and was paired with Cookie, who had already been given extensive training. Andri and her new dog went through a one-week course together at the organization's facility. That was augmented by once-a-week in-home sessions for 13 weeks more. Only when the trainers thought that she and Cookie were ready did Andri get the go-ahead to take her pup out in public.

Three years later, Cookie has more than lived up to Andri's expectations. "Cookie is teaching me how to be deaf," Andri told me. "She reminds me to look twice for cars as I cross the street; to watch out for things behind me; and to *slow down* and be a little more careful."

Andri doesn't have equal hearing loss for all sound frequencies. She can hear bass sounds, so she can hear Cookie bark. But higher pitched, technology-based alerting sounds literally fall on deaf ears. Cookie lets Andri know when the phone or doorbell rings. She alerts to smoke and fire alarms and cars.

"I don't hear from behind me very well," Andri told me. "Cookie is especially vigilant at night. There have been lots of times when people are behind me and I haven't noticed, but Cookie does. She doesn't necessarily have to alert me to every sound when we are out shopping and such. I can simply watch what direction she's looking in, follow her line of vision, and figure out what's going on."

This is even more important because Andri lacks an element of hearing called "echo location." This is what helps us determine the source of a sound. Andri might hear a noise but have no idea where it's coming from. Now Cookie can clue her in—which means, among other things, that she's less likely to get bumped in the market by someone else's shopping cart.

Cookie helps in the kitchen too. She alerts Andri when a timer goes off and has also averted some minor disasters. Once Cookie fetched Andri when some Ramen she'd left boiling and forgotten started foaming. Another time the dog's warning kept a sink from overflowing.

Cookie helps keep Andri safe in many other ways. She alerts when there's someone at the door. One night her barking woke Andri up, and she discovered a woman who was drunk trying to insert her key in Andri's lock. Andri is also less worried now about losing things because she dropped them and didn't hear them fall. These days, if her keys clatter to the ground, Cookie will let her know.

Cookie is a huge help to Andri in navigating the physical world. But she is so much more. This dog has become a social lifeline.

"I have sensorineural hearing loss, which means I have great difficulty understanding speech as well as hearing sound," Andri explained. "Lip reading only gives me about 30 to 60 percent of the conversation. And that's if there are no moustaches to cover the lips and if people speak at proper cadence and don't mumble."

This can be very isolating, especially in family situations and group conversations.

"In order to 'hear' I need one-on-one conversations in a quiet, well-lighted setting," Andri told me. "This is difficult because most conversations happen over mealtimes or in places where there is tremendous background noise and poor lighting. I find myself talking to Cookie a lot. It's just nice to have someone to talk to and not have to worry about struggling to hear their response!"

Cookie also helps build bridges of understanding. Deafness isn't readily apparent by looking at someone. And since Andri's speech is normal, that doesn't serve as a signal either. But Cookie wears a special service-dog vest while she's working. When Andri is out with her dog, people realize she must have a problem. That tends to make them more understanding when she asks for help. And then there is that special brand of Cookie Monster charm.

"Cookie is a beautiful pup—and she knows it," Andri says. "She makes people smile everywhere we go. People, especially kids, take notice of us and ask questions. Cookie seems to make people more friendly."

Andri is deeply grateful for all the ways Cookie has rescued her. Still, Cookie can't make Andri's hearing get better. But God has no such limitations when it comes to our *spiritual* hearing. If we respond to what hearing we have and turn to Him for rescue, He will help us hear more and more clearly over time.

The Bible indicates that sin dulls our spiritual hearing. This was certainly true of the Israelites in Jeremiah's day. In Jeremiah 6:10, the prophet laments,

> To whom can I speak and give warning?
>   Who will listen to me?
> Their ears are closed
>   so they cannot hear.
> The word of the LORD is offensive to them;
>   they find no pleasure in it.

The apostle Paul points out that God's Word can open our spiritual ears to truth. In Romans 10:17 he writes, "Consequently, faith comes from hearing the message, and the message is heard through the word about Christ."

But there's more. Those who give their lives to Jesus receive God's indwelling Holy Spirit. One of His functions is to help us hear God's truth more clearly. And part of that involves spiritual echo location—discerning if something is from God or from someone or someplace else.

One powerful example of this is found in Acts 10. God sent the apostle Peter to a godly Gentile named Cornelius to share the good news with him. A few other Jewish believers tagged along also, and found that Cornelius had gathered his close friends and relatives to listen as well. All these Gentiles believed and were filled with the Spirit. They showed the same indications of this as the apostles had when they were filled with the Spirit at Pentecost. That confirmed to Peter and his friends that not just Jews, but Gentiles too, were to be welcomed into the faith—and it was God saying so. Peter responded by having these new Gentile believers baptized.

Andri knows that Cookie can't help her unless she cooperates. If she ignored her dog's alerts, they wouldn't do her any good. The same goes for us when it comes to spiritual hearing. God speaks to us through His Word and His Spirit and His people, and He uses all of these to fine-tune our hearing over time. But if we neglect to study and pray and listen for His still, small voice, how will we have "ears to hear" what He is saying?

Whether you turn to the right or to the left, your ears will hear a voice behind you, saying, "This is the way; walk in it" (Isaiah 30:21).

CONSIDER THIS:

Do you feel you hear God clearly? Why or why not? Is your spiritual hearing getting better or worse? If it's getting worse, what might you do to cooperate with God so He can give you "ears to hear"?

Mommy's Helper with Fur
Servants Are Saviors

Everybody can be great...because anybody can serve.
You don't have to have a college degree to serve. You don't
have to make your subject and verb agree to serve. You
only need a heart full of grace. A soul generated by love.
Martin Luther King Jr.

If I told you Jodi was drowning and her dog saved her, what image would pop up in your mind's eye? Would you picture a heroic canine hauling a dripping, unconscious human from a large and deep body of water? Well, Jodi was sinking all right, but not in an ocean or lake or the family swimming pool. She was drowning in the details of daily life. She suffers from multiple sclerosis (MS), which can affect balance, movement, vision, hearing, and memory. There are times when Jodi struggles to perform the most mundane of chores, like putting on her socks and doing the laundry. And her devoted assistance dogs have rescued her by helping with those chores—by being her lifeline in the little tasks of living.

Jodi believes she was battling MS long before it was identified. After her first daughter was born, she suffered tremors and was in a wheelchair for a few weeks. Her doctor thought she was just a nervous young mom. But the same thing happened with each of her other two children. Finally, her MS was diagnosed in 1980 when her oldest child was getting ready to go off to college.

It would be 1998 before Jodi got her first assistance dog. She chose a breed not commonly used for this purpose. Sky was a female Harlequin Great Dane—white with black spots. Jodi felt the Great Dane's size and build would give her the kind of support she needed to steady her or ease her to the ground if she lost her balance.

Jodi trained Sky herself and made some of it up as she went. For example, she needed Sky to bring her things, but Great Danes aren't natural retrievers. They play by pulling toys away from each other and won't typically release what they have grabbed. Jodi would hold a toy for Sky to tug and then let go. When Sky looked at her she'd say, "Give it to me."

Sky learned to fetch Jodi's socks and put them on her master's bed. She learned *take* as well as *give* and was able to assist Jodi in putting on or removing certain items of clothing. She learned to put her nose under each of Jodi's ankles and lift her master's feet, one by one.

Sky fetched other items as well. Jodi taught her to open drawers and doors with the help of some specially rigged devices. If Jodi ran out of toilet paper, Sky would open a bathroom cupboard, grab a fresh roll, and take it to her.

Laundry was also on Sky's "Mommy's helper" list. Using a rope with a ball at one end and the other end tied to the clothes basket, Sky learned to pull it where Jodi commanded. Thanks to front-loading appliances and some additional aids rigged to them, Sky was able to help with loading and unloading and to press the start button once Jodi had closed the door and set the time. This team effort between dog and human saved Jodi valuable energy she could then use for other things—like helping to start an assistance dog organization.

Jodi told me that one trick in dog training is to make it feel like a game to the dog. Every now and then, the game backfires. She chuckled when she recalled the peanut butter incident. Sky was nearing the end of her service and was helping to train her successor, another Harlequin Great Dane named Cinder. Cinder couldn't open a cupboard yet, but she loved peanut butter. Sky wasn't mischievous, but Cinder was. So when Jodi found both dogs side by side with brown goo on them, she suspected a group effort.

Jodi came closer and sniffed the goo. Peanut butter. Sure enough, brown goo was oozing from a kitchen cupboard. Inside was a jar of peanut butter with bite holes in it. Apparently Sky opened the cupboard, the dogs got the jar out, and Cinder bit holes in it in her efforts to get at the treat. Then the dogs put the jar back inside and Sky shut the door on the evidence—till the telltale ooze gave them away. Actually, Cinder's efforts to extract peanut butter from the jar had sprayed it around. There was even peanut butter on the kitchen ceiling!

When it came to the Christmas tree, though, it was Jodi who made the mess and Sky who saved the day. The tree was up and beautifully decorated. Jodi was standing back looking at it and decided one Christmas ball was placed wrong. She reached up to fix things—and pulled the whole tree down on herself. She wound up sprawled on the floor, pinned by the fallen tree and surrounded by shattered ornaments.

Sky came running and tried to free her by pulling with her paw on Jodi's shirt. Jodi told Sky, "Get help." Sky knew this meant to get a certain phone and punch a button. This phone had been specially rigged so every button called Jodi's daughter. Sky pressed a button and barked, as she had been taught. Jodi's daughter rushed over and swept up the glass so her mom could be safely extricated.

Jodi felt Sky was God's provision, sent from Him to watch over her. The same was true of Cinder. Cinder's breeder happened to see an article about Sky and contacted Jodi and offered her a dog that could have cost up to five thousand dollars *as a free gift*! Sky assisted in Cinder's training, setting an example of what Cinder should do and nipping Cinder's ear or rear end if the newbie walked too fast. Cinder became a great friend and helper to Jodi also, and learned the names of over two dozen items that she'd fetch on command.

These days Cinder is up in years, and a third dog, Stormy, is in training to take the mantle from her. Both dogs remain devoted to Jodi. Not long ago she had hip replacement surgery and was bedridden for a time. The pair stayed by her bed for two or three weeks.

Jodi's dogs were faithful to come alongside her and give her the help she needed. Many long centuries ago, Moses needed help too. He and his people were in the wilderness. The children of Israel were battling the Amalekites (Exodus 17), and Joshua was ordered to lead the charge while Moses took Aaron and Hur to the top of a hill and held God's staff aloft. As long as he did this, Israel prevailed. But when Moses tired and his arms dropped, Amalek started winning. Seeing this, Aaron and Hur got a big rock for Moses to sit on. Then they stood on either side and each held up one of Moses's arms. That made the prophet's arms steady as a rock and the battle belonged to God's people.

Aaron and Hur were great leaders in their own right, but they were willing to be servants when needed—to literally play a supporting role. Jesus was willing to be a servant too. He is the Son of God and the Messiah, but His first coming to this earth was not in might and power and glory. He was born to humble parents in a town called Bethlehem. He grew up to be a carpenter till, at age 30, He began a three-and-a-half-year ministry that ended in an ignominious death.

Jesus died for our sins in the ultimate act of servanthood. He washed our filthy spiritual laundry white as snow. His arms were held up not by faithful men but by nails driven through His hands into a Roman cross. He defeated sin and death and Satan and was raised by God the Father so that through faith in Him, we could have eternal life.

Sky and Cinder rescued Jodi by being faithful servants. Jesus has done that and more for us. Could there be any higher calling than to humble ourselves and serve others so that they might know His love and rescue too?

Jesus called them together and said, "You know that the rulers of the Gentiles lord it over them, and their high officials exercise authority over them. Not so with you. Instead, whoever wants to become great among you must be your servant, and whoever wants to be first must be

your slave—just as the Son of Man did not come to be served, but to serve, and to give his life as a ransom for many" (Matthew 20:25-28).

CONSIDER THIS:

Who in your life is most servant-like? How has this person served you in significant ways? How did it impact your life? How did it make you feel toward that person? Toward God? How might God want you to love and serve others in His name?

The Scent that Led Under the Snow
Search and Rescue Is God's Business

*There are defining moments in your life where the
road ahead of you takes questionable turns, but
if GOD is your GPS you will never be lost.*
AUTHOR UNKNOWN

Have you ever heard the expression, "It's like looking for a needle in a haystack"? Search and rescue dogs smell for that needle. Golden retriever Zeke was good at it. He had several notable finds—none more remarkable than the discovery of a lost and injured hiker near Yosemite National Park.

Lester Needham and a hiking partner were backpacking together in July 1986. As they headed up a steep canyon in California's Sierra Nevada, they started getting separated. They could see a spot in the distance where they'd be able to join up again, so they agreed to continue on their separate paths. Soon a large outcropping of rock blocked them from each other's view.

Lester chose to cross a snowfield, even though he knew it might be slick. He lost his footing and slid down a slope on his backpack. He slammed into a large boulder sticking out of the snow. The sun had heated up this huge rock and snow had melted around it. Our hapless hiker bounced off the rock and into this meltaway, plummeting some

25 to 30 feet into a snow cave and landing in an icy stream. His backpack bore the brunt of the fall and may have saved his life. But he'd broken his back in the mishap, and one heel and leg too. He was in deep trouble—in more ways than one. Though he somehow managed to drag himself onto a granite shelf, his broken leg was still submerged in the icy stream. There was also a waterfall whose frigid spray kept splattering him with more unwelcome damp and cold.

Meanwhile, when Lester failed to show up, his hiking buddy sounded the alarm. Park officials teamed with adjoining Mono County personnel to launch a coordinated search and rescue effort.

John Dill worked for Yosemite and helped coordinate for them. He explained that such searches were a double-edged sword. If you were going to save someone's life, speed was of the essence. But if you weren't thorough, you might miss a vital clue. So it was that multiple sweeps of an area were done, and a mix of ground searchers, helicopters, and search-dog teams were used.

Enter Zeke and his handler, Marty Cross. They were flown to the top of a ridge and told to search along a creek going downhill through a ravine. This area had already been foot-searched and gone over by helicopters. Marty didn't think it likely he and Zeke would find anything the others hadn't. He thought there were more strategic places to put Zeke's nose to work, such as the missing hiker's Point Last Seen. But he did as he'd been asked.

Marty's job was to make sure Zeke covered as much area as possible. Zeke's job was to sniff the air and ground for human scent. Zeke was trained to latch onto a "scent cone." Scent travels upward and outward from its source in something of a cone shape, like a flashlight beam. If Zeke could find any part of that cone and track it to its starting point, hopefully they'd find their missing man.

Zeke and Marty started bouncing back and forth down the hill, following the stream. They came to a beautiful granite rock canyon. At one point, the stream flowed into a big snow tunnel. Zeke seemed very interested and kept moving. The snow tunnel went into a massive rock formation, and Marty had to detour around it. On the other side he found a huge snowfield. It was the very place where Lester had slipped.

Zeke took off down the snowy slope, and Marty followed, trying to keep up. It seemed the dog was zoning in on something. When Marty realized what it was, he yelled in fear. Zeke was headed for a big hole, and Marty was worried his dog might fall in. Zeke didn't. He stood on the edge of the hole, ears straight up, tail wagging.

Marty was afraid that the snow around the hole could break off under him, so he crawled cautiously up to the edge and looked in. *There was Lester, three stories below him! He had been there three days!*

Marty radioed for a friend and fellow searcher who was close by. This friend had paramedic training, and he went down and evaluated Lester. He and Marty were both amazed that Lester was still alive. It was so cold they had to take turns going down to the hiker and giving him aid while they waited for more help to arrive.

The weather had turned cloudy and stormy. Lester's wife, Mary Jo, recalls that conditions were horrible for a helicopter landing. They were finally able to get a military chopper in. She recalls its code name was *Angel 1*. It hovered just above the ground as Lester was placed on a stretcher and hoisted inside. Though he had to go through a prolonged recovery period and had nerve damage and chronic back pain for the rest of his life, Lester lived for almost 20 years more.

Zeke's story didn't end there either. He had a number of other finds in his distinguished search-and-rescue career. One involved a little girl who somehow got separated from her cousins on the way to a restroom in a campground by Emerald Bay in Lake Tahoe. She was barefoot and had only light clothing on. A search was launched. Zeke and Marty were part of it, and Zeke found her. She'd been headed into the wilderness when he led Marty to her. As a parent, Marty felt special pleasure in reuniting her with her loved ones.

Another time, Zeke and Marty joined a massive search for a lost hunter. This man had a medical history of stroke. Marty was given a well-defined area to search and told not to go beyond it. Suddenly, Zeke had a different idea. He shot down the other side of a fairly steep ridge and led Marty to a creek. The dog got on a rock in pointing position. Marty called the hunter's name and a voice from across the creek yelled for help.

Uplifting as these "live finds" are, there's another side to search-and-rescue work. Sadly, you might find a body instead. One of Zeke's most technically difficult finds was an avalanche victim. This man and his dog had been living in a house in Twin Lakes, California. He'd been warned of high avalanche danger and urged to evacuate, but the man refused to heed the warning. He said he'd stick it out. He said his house had been built to be avalanche-proof.

When the avalanche came, it cut the house off its foundation. That house tumbled 100 yards down a hill and landed at the edge of a lake. Rescuers weren't able to go in for six days due to continued avalanche danger.

Marty and Zeke were part of the search team. Marty explained that in such cases, what a dog alerts to is a faint scent percolating up through the snow. When the dog smells something, the humans start digging.

Zeke alerted, and a crew of men dug all day, encountering a labyrinth of tunnels. As it got dark, the man's dog popped out of the snow alive. Sadly, conditions did not permit the efforts to continue and the diggers had to call it a night. Next day, as Zeke kept alerting, they brought in a snow cat. The snow cat took about 12 to 15 feet of snow off. Zeke went nuts. Further digging uncovered a wooden subfloor. When the searchers chain-sawed through it, they found the missing man in a sleeping bag on a cot—frozen solid.

As I've reflected on Zeke and his escapades, I've been reminded that search and rescue is also very much God's business. He seeks those who are spiritually lost. Peter tells us in 2 Peter 3:9 that "[the Lord] is patient with you, not wanting anyone to perish, but everyone to come to repentance."

Our marvelously merciful God keeps seeking long after we foolish humans might have given up the search. That's how a first-century thief on a cross next to Jesus wound up in the kingdom of God. He had hit bottom. He was dying a horribly painful and ignominious death. He had just heard another dying thief taunt the Lord, but this man summoned his last drop of strength and defended Jesus. Then he looked up through a crack in his snow cave of sin and begged for help. He asked that Jesus remember him when He inherited His kingdom. And Jesus peered into that spiritual hole the man was in and said, "Truly I tell you, today you will be with me in paradise" (Luke 23:43).

Sadly, not all God's searches end in live finds either. Jesus's story about Lazarus and the rich man illustrates this. Lazarus was a starving beggar covered with sores who lay at the rich man's gate. He would have been thrilled with the rich man's table scraps, but the fellow showed him no mercy. Finally Lazarus died and was brought to Abraham by angels. The hard-hearted rich man passed away as well...and landed in torment in Hades. Looking up from the hole he was in, he saw Lazarus with Abraham and asked that the beggar be sent to cool his tongue. Abraham told him it was too late. There was a vast chasm between them that could not be crossed. Then the rich man went to Plan B. Could Abraham send Lazarus to warn his five brothers? Abraham said no. He said they had Moses and the Prophets to do that. And when the rich man pressed him further, Abraham told him, "If they do not listen to Moses and the Prophets, they will not be convinced even if someone rises from the dead" (Luke 16:31).

Zeke had a finite time and place to do his search-and-rescue work. God is outside of time and space. No matter what hole you're in, He will find you if you let Him. And He wants to team with you to search out others lost in a spiritual wilderness and lead them joyfully home.

I waited patiently for the LORD;
  he turned to me and heard my cry.
He lifted me out of the slimy pit,
  out of the mud and mire;
he set my feet on a rock
  and gave me a firm place to stand.
He put a new song in my mouth,
  a hymn of praise to our God.
Many will see and fear the LORD
  and put their trust in him.
                    (Psalm 40:1-3)

CONSIDER THIS:

Have you ever been physically lost and in need of rescue? What scared you most? What comforted you most? How did you get found? Have you ever been found by Jesus? If not, will you let Him find you now?

His Nose Saved Lives

God Smells Dangers We Don't

It is what you don't expect...that most needs looking for.
NEAL STEPHENSON, *Anathem*

As a kid growing up in the fifties, I loved watching a TV show called *The Adventures of Rin Tin Tin*. German shepherd Rinty was a private in the US Cavalry, and his orphan master, Rusty, was a corporal. Boy and dog lived at a fort, were cared for by the soldiers, and helped them keep order in the nineteenth-century Wild West.

It's the twenty-first century now, and the story line has changed. German shepherd Chopper and his military master, Trevor, were deployed overseas. They helped special operations forces steer clear of roadside bombs. Oh, and by the way, this wasn't a fictional tale on TV. It was real life!

This true story began when Trevor chose Chopper from a pool of three dogs. Chopper was about a year and eight months old. Based on the dog's past experience and training, Trevor knew he was apt to be impeccably obedient. Trevor was serving in an elite branch of the military and had applied and been selected for a special program. It involved a unique partnership between human and dog. Normally military dogs are trained in one main specialty. Chopper was taught a smorgasbord of skills. He learned such things as explosives detection, search and rescue, and tracking. Trevor was schooled in these skills too, and in how to train Chopper and understand and meet all his dog's needs.

After many weeks of intensive preparation, Trevor and Chopper were sent to join special ops missions in high-risk areas. They were dropped in and out of various situations to smell out danger and forestall calamities.

Trevor told me the highest threat in these areas was from roadside bombs, also known as improvised explosive devices (IEDs). Chopper was trained to detect them and would indicate the danger by his body language. Trevor understood his dog's cues and would get his companions out of the way or have qualified personnel deal with the device, depending on the circumstances. Chopper repeatedly saved his humans from being maimed or killed.

Chopper could also detect an ambush before it happened. Trevor remembers one incident in particular. The bad guys were hiding in a cave about 25 yards ahead and below where Trevor and Chopper and their companions were advancing. There were multiple would-be attackers and they had some powerful weapons. Chopper's human companions neither saw nor heard the threat. Chopper literally smelled trouble and reacted as he had been trained. Had that not happened, Trevor believes they all would have been killed. Instead, they lived to tell the tale and reward Chopper with a steak—well seasoned with gratitude.

In another situation, Trevor was attempting to take a prisoner, but the fellow wouldn't put his hands up. Then he darted into a building. Usually that meant a bomb would be launched or bullets sprayed at those outside. Chopper went in and kept the fellow from attacking until Trevor could get inside and capture him.

Chopper's activities bring to mind how God and His chosen servants seek to guide and warn us. We live in a fallen world and are in constant danger from roadside bombs of temptation. Sin lurks, waiting to ambush us when we least expect it. And even when we try to take it prisoner, it may refuse to surrender, taking cover and seeking to fire on us instead.

An Old Testament leader named Joshua tried to warn his people of a roadside bomb just before leading them to victory over Jericho. God had decreed that everything in the city was His. Most of it was to be burned. Precious metals were excluded, but were reserved for God Himself. This wise leader knew the lure of plunder and the explosive consequences disobedience would have. In Joshua 6:18-19 (msg), he urged, "As for you, watch yourselves in the city under holy curse. Be careful that you don't covet anything in it and take something that's cursed, endangering the camp of Israel with the curse and making trouble for everyone. All silver and gold, all vessels of bronze and iron are holy to God. Put them in God's treasury."

Sadly, not everyone handled this temptation as Joshua had directed. A man named Achan stole a gorgeous robe and some gold and silver. Sure enough, the Israelites lost their very next battle and 36 men were killed. Only after the culprit was smoked out and dealt with according to God's commands was His protection over the people restored (Joshua 7).

An example of someone who *did* heed God's warnings was the apostle Paul. That's how he saved the lives of all those with him when he was shipwrecked (Acts 27). Paul had been taken prisoner, and he and a few other captives were being sent to Rome. Against Paul's advice, the Roman centurion in charge decided to set sail from Crete at a stormy time of year. Sure enough, they got caught up in bad weather and were tossed around in the sea like a cork. Everyone but Paul thought they were doomed. But God told Paul otherwise. God revealed that Paul must stand before Caesar, and although they would be shipwrecked, every life would be spared.

Paul believed God and gave this news to everyone else aboard. Still, some of the sailors were ambushed by fear. They planned to jump in a lifeboat and take off. Paul realized what was happening and warned the centurion and his men that if the sailors didn't stay put, everyone's life would be lost.

The centurion heeded Paul's warning. His men cut the boat loose so the sailors couldn't flee. Everyone ate to keep their strength up, as Paul urged them to. And the centurion didn't allow any prisoners to be killed. As a result, every single one of those on board survived, and Paul went to Rome to stand trial, just as God said he would.

Chopper saved his humans multiple times because they paid attention to him. Trevor was trained to recognize Chopper's alerts. He responded instantly, as did those with him, and they were rescued from untold grief and death.

How much more all-knowing and loving and wise is our awesome God? How much more does He yearn to rescue us from spiritual harm? Will you train yourself to recognize the warnings in His Word and through His Spirit so He can keep you safe in Him?

Do not quench the Spirit. Do not treat prophecies with contempt but test them all; hold on to what is good, reject every kind of evil (1 Thessalonians 5:19-22).

CONSIDER THIS:

When was the last time God helped you dodge a spiritual roadside bomb in your life? What happened? How did you avoid the threat? What did you learn? Are there areas of your life where you need to pay closer attention to God's alerts?

Who Rescued Whom?
God Knows What We Need

*Each of us may be sure that if God sends us on stony paths
He will provide us with strong shoes, and He will not send us
out on any journey for which He does not equip us well.*
ALEXANDER MACLAREN

I first met Caleb at a wedding reception. He was escorting one of the bridesmaids. This would not have been remarkable except—Caleb is a dog.

Actually, Caleb is a service dog. His master, Pamela, suffers from some rare health conditions, one of which used to cause her to collapse without warning. Caleb would sense when such an episode was coming and would alert her.

If you're wondering how Caleb was taught to do this—he wasn't! He did it all on his own. In fact, when Pamela and her husband, Jay, took Caleb in, it was not to rescue her. It was to rescue the dog.

Pamela's health issues keep her home a lot. Jay's fire captain duties keep him away. His shifts are 24 hours long. Still, when someone suggested a service dog, Pamela rejected the notion. She had a cat for company, and a dog seemed like too much work. Even when she caught an episode of a popular dog-training show and found herself fascinated, she resisted the concept of a canine companion.

God had other ideas.

It was Jay who decided they would take in a seven-month-old rescue dog. *Fine, till we find it another home,* Pamela thought. The homeless pooch was a gorgeous white Korean jindo with a peach tail and ears. He was terrified of people and shook when they looked at him. They dubbed him Caleb and are delighted that he has become brave and bold just like his Old Testament namesake.

Caleb was terrified of human touch, so Pamela gave him his space. She sensed he needed time to trust his new people. So it surprised her when, a few days into their relationship, Caleb was the one to initiate contact.

Pamela was stretched out on the sofa reading, with Caleb on the couch by her feet. She felt nature calling, and as she moved to rise, Caleb placed his front paws on her calves, pressed down, and stared intently into her eyes.

Pamela's first impulse was to wonder if the dog was trying to tell her something. Shrugging the idea off as silly, she stood up. Instantly, she crumpled to the ground. Fortunately, her head missed the glass coffee table.

When she was able, Pamela struggled back onto the sofa. Eventually she told Caleb she had to get up. She was sitting, then she was almost standing. Did he have any reaction to this? Caleb didn't. He ignored the whole thing. Pamela went to the bathroom. No problem.

From that moment, Pamela knew that Caleb knew. She believes her dog was (and is) God's provision. He seems able to pick up on changes in her body that signal trouble, and he has the heart to warn her. She has learned to listen.

Caleb quickly learned his name and basic commands. One of them was *bring*, which he did with his favorite stuffed toy. On another evening, Pamela was again home alone and reading on the couch when she was hit with brutal pain. Normally she senses it coming, but this time it was sudden and excruciating. She saw her pain pills out of reach on the coffee table, but there was no way she could get to them. The pain was too much for her. She asked the Lord what to do, and He turned her eyes to Caleb.

"I was dubious, but it was worth a shot," Pamela recalls. "I pointed at the bottle of pills and said, 'Bring pills.' Caleb looked where I was pointing and back at me, a bit uncertain. 'Bring pills,' I urged again. He jumped off the sofa, trotted to the coffee table, and turned to me for assurance. 'Yes! Bring pills.' He touched the bottle with his nose and looked at me again. 'Yes, yes, good boy! Bring pills.' He nosed the bottle off the table, carefully picked it up in his mouth, and jumped back on the sofa beside me. After a stunned moment, I thought, *Okay, we're keeping this dog.* He hasn't left my side since."

Caleb has rescued Pamela not just from physical pain and harm, but also from isolation. She feels safer going out knowing she has Caleb to alert her of an impending problem. She recalls one evening, early in this new adventure, when she thought she was fine—but Caleb sensed otherwise.

She and Jay had gone to see friends. Caleb suddenly rose and stared at her. When she looked back, he turned toward the door, took some steps in place, and gazed intently back into her eyes. She knew he was prodding her to leave, but she didn't want to. She asked Jay to see if Caleb needed to relieve himself. Nope, that wasn't it. Still resisting, she told her hosts she should go before overdoing it, but good-byes dragged on for another 15 or 20 minutes. Meantime Caleb was growing more and more antsy. Finally they were in the car, with Jay driving. Pamela felt severe pain about 15 minutes before they reached home. She was amazed to realize if she'd left when Caleb wanted, she would have made it back before things got bad. Subsequent incidents confirmed the dog's uncanny sense of timing.

Pamela wrote me, "In the beginning, I thought we were rescuing a poor, abused dog, but the truth was that he was sent to rescue me. James 1:17 says, 'Every good and perfect gift is from above, coming down from the Father of the heavenly lights.' Caleb is my good and perfect gift from God that I didn't know I needed."

Jeremiah the prophet was Judah's good and perfect gift from God that the Israelites didn't know they needed. God sent him to warn a rebellious, idolatrous nation. Though some listened, others didn't even *want* to hear the message that severe pain was coming because they refused to seek the Lord and worship Him only. Jeremiah warned of

Jerusalem's destruction and the exile of Judah's citizens as God's judgment against wickedness and spiritual harlotry. Jeremiah's words came true, and the 70-year Babylonian captivity followed.

Though this exile was the farthest thing from rescue, as far as the Israelites were concerned, it was just that from God's perspective. He was disciplining His people to save them from something far worse—their sin. God was also spreading them among pagan peoples so that the Gentiles might see Him at work and some might come to faith.

Jeremiah's prophecies offered rescue from despair as well. Judgment would be followed by restoration. In Jeremiah 29:10-14 we read,

> This is what the LORD says: "When seventy years are completed for Babylon, I will come to you and fulfill my good promise to bring you back to this place. For I know the plans I have for you," declares the LORD, "plans to prosper you and not to harm you, plans to give you hope and a future. Then you will call on me and come and pray to me, and I will listen to you. You will seek me and find me when you seek me with all your heart. I will be found by you," declares the LORD, "and will bring you back from captivity. I will gather you from all the nations and places where I have banished you," declares the LORD, "and will bring you back to the place from which I carried you into exile."

This prophecy had a "near fulfillment" when Jerusalem and the temple were rebuilt, as recorded in the books of Ezra and Nehemiah. Many believe these words also point to a "far fulfillment"—in the end times. And indeed, the nation of Israel was reestablished in 1948 after nearly 1900 years, and Jews have come there from all over the world. Could this be a step in the fulfillment of other end-times prophecies culminating in Jesus's Second Coming? Many believe so.

In vastly different ways, Caleb the dog and Jeremiah the prophet were instruments of God sent to warn and rescue His children. But for that rescue to happen, people had to *hear* the warning and *heed* it. I believe God longs to rescue each of us in big and little ways all the time—if we will only listen for His guidance, trust, and obey.

"Now, son of man, I am making you a watchman for the people of Israel. Therefore, listen to what I say and warn them for me" (Ezekiel 33:7 NLT).

CONSIDER THIS:

How has God alerted you to physical or spiritual peril in your life? Did you heed the warning or ignore it? What was the result? How might you be even more alert and responsive to God in the future?

Part II

A Helping Paw in Trouble

Nugget

Saved by the Bark
Love Endures Rejection

You can't live a perfect day without doing something
for someone who will never be able to repay you.
JOHN WOODEN

Vilma's family might be more inclined to say "saved by the bark" than "saved by the bell." The bark in question belongs to a wonderful bichon frise/poodle mix named Nugget, whose kindness in the face of rejection turned him into a savior.

Vilma's young daughter had been begging for a dog for Christmas, but Vilma was concerned that a dog might be too much to handle. She was working on her PhD, and she also had two children to care for. And the family went to visit her husband's relatives in Germany every summer. What would they do with a dog then? What would they do with one, period? Maybe they ought to get a cat. A cat was less labor-intensive, and less work made more sense, right?

Not in God's all-encompassing wisdom. I still remember the morning I prayed with Vilma, asking for God's guidance in her pet selection. She went to visit some rescue cats later that day. It didn't feel right. She felt a tug to go to the local animal shelter. She found Nugget, and he grabbed her heart.

In the months that followed, Nugget grabbed her son's and daughter's and husband's hearts too. He brought the whole family together. He soothed stress just by his loving presence and helped forge a closer bond between a brother and his much younger sister. But his deepest rescue work was yet to come. That work involved Vilma's ailing mother.

Vilma is from Guatemala, where her mom was still living. But her health was going downhill, and so it wasn't long before she came to live with Vilma's family. Three years earlier, in her homeland, she had been badly bitten by a big dog. That dog had not been vaccinated for rabies, and Vilma's mom was forced to endure a painful series of shots. This experience left her deeply fearful of *all* dogs, even friendly little Nugget.

Vilma was forced to put up a baby gate and restrict Nugget to the kitchen and a study room. That way her mom could be dog-free in the rest of the house. Nugget sensed her dislike but responded with kindness. He would sit behind the gate and look at her as she rested on the living room couch. Vilma's mom was battling cancer. She was frail and used a walker. She couldn't do much. Gradually, Nugget became her entertainment.

In time, Nugget also became the older woman's comforter and protector. He had different barks for different people and situations. Vilma had hired a caregiver to help with her mom, and the caregiver had a key. Nugget had a special, friendly bark to announce the caregiver's arrival. This was different from his "stranger bark." Vilma's mom couldn't get out of bed by herself at this point. She couldn't see who was coming in the door. But she could hear Nugget's telltale bark and it gave her peace of mind.

Sadly, the cancer spread to the brain, and Vilma's mom needed chemotherapy. There was scar tissue. She started having seizures. Then, she suffered a stroke and almost died. As she recovered, she had to learn to walk and talk again. Initially, she lost much of her memory. Maybe she forgot the dog bite incident back in Guatemala. She seemed warmer toward Nugget than before. Even when more of her memory returned, her kindness toward Nugget persisted. She would even give him treats.

About a year after the stroke, Vilma's mom started having grand mal seizures. They were so severe that she couldn't move for a couple of hours afterward. In the beginning, they happened about once a month, though there was no way to predict them—or so Vilma thought.

A caregiver was the first to realize that Nugget apparently sensed something his people couldn't. About a minute before a seizure, Nugget became restless. He let out a weird bark. This dog somehow knew something was wrong and was alerting his humans.

Nugget's alert was a huge assist. The caregiver could get Vilma's mom into a safer place or position. The caregiver also found comfort in having a tiny window of time to prepare for what was to happen. This became even more significant when the seizures increased to two or three a week, and sometimes two in a row.

Eventually, things got so bad with her mom that Vilma was forced to move her into a nursing home. She had severe dementia and was losing her memory again. A therapist told Vilma it would comfort her mom to have familiar pictures in her room. The one photo Vilma's mom specifically asked for was a picture of Nugget.

Nugget's persistent love and care, even in the face of rejection, makes me think of God's love and care for us. Romans 5:10 (NLT) puts it this way: "For since our friendship with God was restored by the death of his Son while we were still his enemies, we will certainly be saved through the life of his Son."

Such sacrificial, enduring love is beautifully pictured in the Old Testament by Moses's shepherding of the Israelites. God used Moses to free them from slavery, lead them out of Egypt, give them His Ten Commandments and laws, and take them to the very edge of the Promised Land. But there were times when they felt more bitten than rescued by this amazing prophet, and they repaid his kindness with rejection.

One such time was before they even made it out of Egypt. Moses was confronting Pharaoh, God was bringing plagues on Egypt, and the Egyptians were taking out their anger on the Hebrew slaves. The Egyptians had been giving them straw to meet their daily quota of bricks. Pharaoh ordered the straw dole stopped—but insisted they still meet their daily brick count. They couldn't, and the Hebrew foremen took a drubbing for it. They felt bitten and said as much to Moses and his brother, Aaron: "May GOD see what you've done and judge you—you've made us stink before Pharaoh and his servants! You've put a weapon in his hand that's going to kill us!" (Exodus 5:21 MSG). This situation made Moses doubt the course of action God had him on— till God reassured him His people would go free.

There isn't space to record all the other ways Moses persevered in the face of rejection. But one further parallel with Nugget is worth noting. Moses, like the faithful prophets who would follow, alerted his people to a list of blessings if they worshipped God alone and kept His commands and a list of curses if they fell into idolatry and sin. Those curses, Moses warned, would culminate in a "grand mal" judgment—they would be conquered and exiled from the Promised Land. *But*, even in the midst of judgment, God used Moses to rescue His people from despair. Moses foretold God's promise that He would gather a remnant and restore them to the land one day.

Nugget and Moses showed love and care to those who pushed them away. By so doing, they became instruments of rescue. Does God want to use you like this too? We can't always fathom His ways, but He will give us eyes to see if we ask with an open heart.

Moses went back to GOD and said, "My Master, why are you treating this people so badly? And why did you ever send me? From the moment I came to Pharaoh to speak in your name, things have only gotten worse for this people. And rescue? Does this look like rescue to you?"

GOD said to Moses, "Now you'll see what I'll do to Pharaoh: With a strong hand he'll send them out free; with a strong hand he'll drive them out of his land" (Exodus 5:22–6:1 MSG).

CONSIDER THIS:

Has God ever led you to love and care for someone who "bit" you instead of thanking you? Did you persevere? Did their heart change? What did God teach you?

A Doggie to Lean On

Gentle Is as Gentle Loves

Nothing is so strong as gentleness,
nothing so gentle as real strength.
Francis de Sales

Ug the chow chow didn't seem like a dog that would come to someone's rescue. It seemed more likely that someone would need rescuing from him. Though he adored his household of humans, he could be a nightmare for strangers or those he *considered* strangers.

Judy was ten when her dad brought the chow puppy home to join the family. Judy's mom chose the name Ug—possibly because she wasn't consulted about the new four-footed addition. As Ug matured, he grew into a gorgeous physical specimen and became a great pal to Judy, listening patiently as she poured out her thoughts to him. It was a different story with outsiders. Ug guarded his backyard so zealously that he wouldn't even let family friends into his domain.

Ug's activities didn't stop there—despite the six-foot fence. He learned to scale it at will. When Judy's dad chained him to a stake, he broke free and came home bloody from fighting. Ug proceeded to conquer a whole series of progressively stronger chains. The one that finally held him was used to pull trucks. But useful as this chain was with Ug, it was hazardous to humans. Judy and her brother ran afoul of it playing and took a number of spills when the chain got wrapped around their feet. They learned to be ever watchful of it, but they were glad it kept Ug home safe—and kept others safe from him.

That was why Judy's heart landed in her throat one Saturday afternoon when she saw a neighbor girl venture into the yard. This little five-year-old had had polio and needed heavy metal braces and crutches to walk. Even so, she was unsteady as she lurched laboriously along, swinging one leg forward at a time—wobbling straight for Ug!

Judy raced to save the child. No saving needed! The little girl had grabbed hold of Ug's ruff and was chattering away. He listened patiently—just as he did with Judy. Then, still hanging on to Ug, the child leaned over and picked up a piece of bone. It was circular with a hole in the middle. She stuck the bone on her finger and tried to feed it to the dog. Ug kept his mouth closed at first. But after she'd poked him with it several times, he took her offering. She explained proudly to Judy that she liked to feed him bones—and he liked it too.

Ug dropped the bone. Not to be deterred, the child hung on to his mane, retrieved it, and fed it to him again. This time she also fed him a lecture about how he ought to be polite and take it when she gave it. His response was to walk a little distance away, and then drop the bone again.

The little girl lurched toward the bone and stumbled over Ug's chain. Ug was watching and saw her fall. When she called him, he came and stood beside her. Judy watched wide-eyed as he stiffened and braced himself. The child grabbed on to Ug and literally used the dog to pull herself upright, yanking the skin on his spine clear down to his belly.

Hanging on to Ug's ruff for balance, the child retrieved the bone once more. Ug took it from her, and this time he held on to it. Not until she left the yard did he drop the bone. Then he came to Judy and dropped his head in her lap. As she caressed him, he heaved a huge sigh.

From that time, whenever the little neighbor girl came into the yard, Ug would let her feed him a bone. He would also watch to see if she was in danger of falling. If so, he would brace her with his body. And if she did trip on his chain, he would go to her and let her pull herself up with his skin.

It was not until decades later, when Judy shared Ug's story with me, that she realized its full impact on her. She'd always seen Ug as God's gift and provision. But, all these years later, she now realized her dog was also used by God to plant a powerful insight deep within her. Ug was a doggie illustration and parable of strength and power used ever so gently to rescue one in need.

Ug's story fairly shouted to my heart and mind as well. I thought of how an infinitely more powerful God deals with us when we stumble and fall. I thought of how He restrains His power and gently and patiently comes alongside us and lets us grab on to Him.

Many long centuries ago, Moses experienced God's gentle rescue. As a baby, his Hebrew mother had placed him in a basket on the Nile because Egypt's king had decreed all male Hebrew babies be killed. Pharaoh's daughter found and adopted him. Moses was raised in Pharaoh's court as a prince, but he knew his Hebrew origins. When a grown-up Moses saw an Egyptian beating a Hebrew slave, he took it upon himself to kill the man and hide his body. Moses wasn't exactly a poster boy for gentle rescue—at least not then.

This deed did not remain hidden. It became known to other Hebrews and to Pharaoh, who wanted Moses dead. Moses fled to Midian, married a priest's daughter, and became a shepherd. Many long years passed. The old Pharaoh died. Things were getting worse for the children of Israel, and they begged God for rescue. God heard. And one day in Midian, He appeared to Moses in a burning bush (Exodus 3).

Moses had seemingly learned a few things in those intervening years. He wasn't quite so rash and brash anymore. When God announced He'd selected Moses to rescue His people, Moses's first response was, "Who am I that I should go to Pharaoh and bring the Israelites out of Egypt?" (Exodus 3:11).

God had an answer. Moses's sufficiency wasn't the issue here. God would be with him and work through him to get the job done.

You'd have thought that would be enough. Hadn't Moses just seen a bush that was on fire but not consumed? Nevertheless, Moses kept shoving objections at God like that little girl shoved that bone at Ug. What if the people asked him God's name? What if they didn't believe God had sent him?

God could have lost His temper with Moses. He could have obliterated His unwilling prophet. But He was patient and gentle instead. He answered Moses's questions and gave him signs and wonders to perform to validate his commission. God recognized that Moses had tripped on the chain of unbelief, and He was offering him aids to pull himself up.

No go! Moses voiced his final objection. "Pardon your servant, Lord. I have never been eloquent…I am slow of speech and tongue" (Exodus 4:10). God gently pointed out that He was the author of speech. He (God) could handle this!

Even if God could, Moses couldn't. He begged God to send someone else.

This got God angry. Scripture says His anger "burned." But He didn't strike Moses dead or withdraw His request. He gave His reluctant servant yet one more aid to grab on to—his brother, Aaron. Moses would tell Aaron what to say, and Aaron would be his mouthpiece.

Moses stopped objecting. He grabbed on to God's offer and pulled himself up. He let God use him to lead the Israelites out of Egypt. And when they tripped on the chain of unbelief and worshipped a golden calf, Moses interceded with God and begged for their lives. He went on to become one of the Bible's greatest prophets.

Why a chow that could be a nightmare had a dream response to a physically challenged child is something we can only guess. But we *know* why God responded as He did. He knows what is in each of our hearts and minds. He understands and has compassion on our weakness. And He loves us with an unconditional, everlasting love. His goal is not to crush us but to save us.

God also knows the hurts and needs of those who cross our path. He knows who in our lives needs gentle rescue. And if we will seek His wisdom and listen to His still, small voice, we can be His instruments… just as Ug was.

You have also given me the shield of Your salvation,
And Your right hand upholds me;
And Your gentleness makes me great.
                              (Psalm 18:35 NASB)

CONSIDER THIS:

How have you experienced gentle rescue from God? In what
ways has it ministered to you? How have you experienced it
from others? In what ways might God be calling you to be
restrained and gentle in coming alongside and helping some-
one else?

Dog Nanny Knows Best
Some Things Must Be Fled

When a child is locked in the bathroom
with water running and he says he's doing
nothing but the dog is barking, call 911.
ERMA BOMBECK

When my friend Sean was growing up in rural New York, his family eventually numbered twelve kids. For the first ten, their dog Husky was a four-footed nanny. Husky got his name from his breed—he was a Siberian husky. Sean's parents got him just before his oldest sister, Mary, was born. He became the children's self-appointed guardian, and he gave it his doggie all.

Mary remembers Husky joining her when she hid behind the couch during thunderstorms. She thinks he was trying to protect her. He did the same for all the kids as the family expanded. Husky was on high alert when they swam in the lake. Their mom was usually on the beach with a baby, so Husky made it his job to keep the rest safe in the water. He would paddle out past the furthest child and circle his brood like a mother hen in dog fur, swimming laps. As the kids got out of the water, he'd come in closer, but he wouldn't leave the water till the last child was safely on dry land. He also swam alongside the family's boat when they took it out fishing.

Husky watched out for his charges on dry land too. He was always with them when they went sledding. He wouldn't come in the house until all the children were safely inside. That's how Mary found a younger brother the day he broke his collarbone. She retraced her steps and found Husky lying with the boy where he had fallen.

Another hat that Husky wore was that of traffic cop. If his charges headed for the road, he ran ahead. He would look both ways and bark if it wasn't safe to proceed. If it was, he'd trot part way into the road and stop. The children would then cross under his watchful eye. Only after they had done so would he follow.

Husky's self-chosen purpose in life was to keep his humans safe. He was constantly on doggie danger patrol. But never was his role in this more outstanding, or more dramatic, than on the day of the fire.

To the best of Sean's recollection, Husky was outside when the fire was discovered. He stood watch at the door as the family bailed. Sean thinks an older sibling tried to pull the dog away, but he was having none of it. He was not about to budge until he knew everyone had gotten out…and he was allowing one-way traffic only.

There was a lot of confusion and running around. In the midst of it all, the phone rang. Sean's mom, doubtless dazed and on autopilot, tried to go back inside to answer. Husky blocked her way! Sean's mother tried to pull the dog aside, but Husky stood his ground.

One of Sean's brothers grabbed her. What was she thinking? They had to get out of there! Sean's mom snapped to her senses. The family fled the fire. The house didn't totally burn to the ground, but it was pretty much gutted and had to be torn down and rebuilt.

Mulling this over in my own mind decades later, I realized Husky's rescue efforts had several layers. In an immediate and physical way, Husky saved his human from possible injury or death. He also saved the rest of the family from the trauma of such an occurrence. But Husky also rescued Sean's mom from her own temporarily unreliable impulses. Her knee-jerk instinct to go back in and answer the phone was a very bad idea. She needed to take her loved ones and flee.

So did Lot's wife.

We read the story of Lot and his family in the book of Genesis. Lot was Abraham's nephew. At a certain point, the pair split up because their flocks were too large and needed separate grazing. Lot got first choice of where to live and chose the city of Sodom. Sadly, it proved to be a very evil place. Things eventually got so bad that God considered destroying the area completely.

God revealed this to Abraham. Abraham begged God to spare the city if there were even just a few righteous folks there. He entered into a negotiation with God, starting with fifty righteous people being enough to spare Sodom and ending with ten. Sadly the two angels sent to Sodom didn't find even ten good people—just Lot himself, who was assaulted as he tried to protect the angels from being savaged by the townsfolk.

The angels struck their would-be attackers blind. Then they told Lot to take his loved ones and flee. His two daughters' fiancés wouldn't heed his warning. Genesis 19:15-17 (MSG) recounts what followed.

> At break of day, the angels pushed Lot to get going, "Hurry. Get your wife and two daughters out of here before it's too late and you're caught in the punishment of the city."
>
> Lot was dragging his feet. The men grabbed Lot's arm, and the arms of his wife and daughters—GOD was so merciful to them!—and dragged them to safety outside the city. When they had them outside, Lot was told, "Now run for your life! Don't look back! Don't stop anywhere on the plain—run for the hills or you'll be swept away."

Lot didn't like that idea at all. He begged permission to run with his family to a small nearby town called Zoar instead. His request was granted. Once they had reached this refuge, God rained destruction down on Sodom and also Gomorrah. "But Lot's wife looked back and turned into a pillar of salt" (19:26 MSG).

Lot's wife looked back! After all the warnings and all of God's mercy and all of His efforts to pull her away and block her from destruction, she looked back—and it was her undoing.

Which makes me wonder—what is God trying to rescue us from that we insist on looking back at or running back to?

Sean's mother usually knew better than to enter a burning building. But at one critical moment, her instincts failed her. That one moment might have been her undoing—but for a faithful dog.

We don't know much about Lot's wife, but the overall situation suggests her actions were much more intentional. Maybe there were things about her past life that she just couldn't quite let go of to follow God... and they did, indeed, destroy her!

So, what about the things in our lives that are pulling us toward destruction, that we need to turn from and flee? We may not have a dog or an angel to block our path or pull us away, but if we have given our lives to Jesus, we have God's Holy Spirit. He indwells us. He is our spiritual nanny to guide, protect, and teach us. Unlike Husky, He never sleeps and He has all knowledge and power. He is eager to rescue us from both the momentary wrong impulses and the much more entrenched stumbling blocks in our life—if we will let Him. So learn to listen for His voice, follow Him, and don't look back!

Forgetting what is behind and straining toward what is ahead, I press on toward the goal to win the prize for which God has called me heavenward in Christ Jesus (Philippians 3:13-14).

CONSIDER THIS:

What in your life has God warned you to turn from that could destroy you? Did you obey, or look back? What was the result? Is there something God is calling you to flee right now? If you're struggling, have you asked Him to help you?

Life Preserver with Paws
God Rescues Through Us

Use me, God. Show me how to take who I am,
who I want to be, and what I can do, and
use it for a purpose greater than myself.
MARTIN LUTHER KING JR.

Bogie was a marvelous female German shepherd who belonged to the Allyn family. She was six or seven years old when she became part of an amazing God-shaped miracle.

Bill and Penny Allyn were at their summer home in a small, upstate New York town. It was a beautiful cabin overlooking a spring-fed lake. On this June day the water temperature was chilly—probably 65 degrees or colder. They were cooking breakfast for their youngest son, Mark, and some of his buddies. They were also watching their two-year-old grandson, Noah.

Noah was right there with the rest of the family. Then, suddenly, they realized their grandson was gone. They raced outside but didn't see him. Their immediate nightmare scenario was that the toddler would wander into the lake and drown.

Bill called 911. He urged them to send help, including what was needed for underwater rescue. Penny asked Mark and his friends to start searching too. At some point, the family realized that Bogie was also missing. This had never happened before. They had an electronic fence and their dog had never breached it—until now.

All these years later, memories differ. What the family does agree on is that Noah was missing for about 45 minutes. At some point, Mark spied Bogie from the end of the Allyn's dock—and possibly Noah too. They were some distance away, near the lake. Bill leaped into his car and raced to the spot. They also got a call from someone saying they had seen a toddler running with a German shepherd.

When Bill reached Bogie, she was standing between Noah and the water. Noah was throwing stones over Bogie's back. A woman nearby said she'd seen Bogie blocking Noah from going onto the docks.

There was more. To reach this location, boy and dog would have had to travel through a densely wooded and swampy area near the highway. There were deep gullies and one spot where a plank was laid across a creek. This was a journey fraught with peril for a toddler. Bill and Penny believe Bogie must have guided Noah and kept him safe.

In the case of the Allyn family, God used a caring dog to protect and save a human child. In the case of Jews exiled to Persia many long centuries ago, God used an initially reluctant young woman to prevent a mass extermination.

The place was Persia. The time was the Babylonian captivity. The life preserver of God's choosing was a beautiful young Hebrew woman named Esther. Through a series of circumstances, the Persian king, Xerxes, chose Esther to be his new queen. However, he did not know she was Jewish.

Haman, the highest official in the empire, was plotting to have all the Jews in the kingdom killed. Esther's cousin, Mordecai, begged her to speak with the king. But at first she hesitated. If she went to the king without being summoned, she could be put to death. Mordecai responded with the now-famous words,

> "Do not think that because you are in the king's house you alone of all the Jews will escape. For if you remain silent at this time, relief and deliverance for the Jews will arise from

another place, but you and your father's family will perish. And who knows but that you have come to your royal position for such a time as this?" (Esther 4:13-14).

Esther asked that the Jews fast and pray for her. She and her maids also fasted and prayed. God gave her favor with the king, the Jews were spared, and Haman was hanged.

I believe Bogie and Esther were both used by God for "such a time as this." I believe He has special things for each of us to do. In big and small ways, He calls all of us to minister to one another. He could choose to act directly, but instead He allows us the privilege of participating with Him. Will you pray and ask how He might choose to use you even today to be an instrument of His rescue and love?

For we are God's handiwork, created in Christ Jesus to do good works, which God prepared in advance for us to do (Ephesians 2:10).

CONSIDER THIS:

Is there a person or pet God has used in a special, and perhaps surprising, way in your life? What happened? How did it bless you? How did it strengthen your faith? How might God want to use you in someone else's life today?

The Paws that Protected
Watchful to Save

For he hears the lambs innocent call.
And he hears the ewes tender reply.
He is watchful while they are in peace.
For they know when their Shepherd is nigh.

WILLIAM BLAKE

My friend Martha was an only child in the two-footed sense. But in her early years she had an older, four-footed "sibling"—a marvelous boxer named Von Bielski who was both a beloved pal and her special canine guardian angel.

Von's protective duties peaked when Martha was two or three years old. She and her parents were living in Omaha, Nebraska. Little Martha had a bed with rails, but being a bright, energetic, and enterprising toddler, she quickly learned to climb over them. She did this so many times her parents gave up on those rails altogether as a way of keeping Martha out of trouble.

Martha's parents could do this because they knew that when Martha launched out of bed early on a weekend morning as they slept, their faithful dog would be right beside her. Von spent his nights in the child's room. When she arose, so did he. Von was little Martha's shadow. He stayed glued to her as she padded downstairs, played with pots and pans, climbed up to the counter for crackers, and headed out in search of new adventures.

The little wanderer would toddle off to the garage, the sandbox, and other people's backyards to play. She would shed her slippers and robe along the way. But she was never able to shed her dog. Von followed everywhere. He kept strangers away from his charge. He would not permit Martha to cross the street. He would not allow her to leave the neighborhood. If she was headed for such dangers, he would plant his muscular boxer body in front of her, block her way, and growl. Martha's parents were not around to watch Von wrangle their child, but neighbors saw and told them all about it.

Since all this was going on while Martha's parents slept, they had no idea where she was when they woke up. And back in the day, they didn't have a tracking device they could put on their daughter. They weren't troubled, though. They knew how to retrieve her. Martha's mom would call her name, Von would hear, grab the little girl's sleeve, and drag her back home.

Von also stepped in, literally, to save Martha from anyone in her life he perceived as a problem. He was apparently none too fond of Martha's paternal grandmother. He considered it his duty to keep the two apart. If she tried to approach her granddaughter, he would insert himself between them, push Martha back with his rear end, and growl at Granny.

Over half a century later, Martha credits her beloved Von with helping her survive her childhood mostly in one piece. Von, however, did not, given his much shorter life span. Fortunately, Martha invited a new Protector into her life who will be with her and watch over her forever—God!

There is, of course, an infinite difference between a canine guardian and a divine one. But it's intriguing to consider some parallels. Von was loving. He was faithful. He was vigilant. He let Martha wander, but he always brought her home. These are all aspects of God's care for us. Martha has seen this in her life, and the Bible has marvelous examples too, including the story of a pivotal time in the life of Jacob, one of Israel's patriarchs.

When this part of his story begins, Jacob was a grown man physically. Spiritually, it was quite a different matter. He didn't seem to get who God was. He was a conniving opportunist who, at his mother's urging, tricked his elderly father into giving him a highly significant blessing that rightfully belonged to his twin brother, Esau, as the eldest son.

Esau was furious. He was ready to kill Jacob…literally. He figured their father, Isaac, would die soon. After that, he'd take his revenge. Their mother got wind of this and decided to send Jacob far away till Esau's anger cooled. She told her husband she wanted Jacob to go back to her homeland and take a wife from there, instead of marrying a local Canaanite woman. Isaac agreed, and Jacob was sent off to his mother's family in Paddan Aram.

Just as Von stepped in to save Martha from dangers she didn't even realize were there, God stepped in and promised He would keep Jacob safe. He appeared to Jacob in a dream. He repeated the covenant He had made with Jacob's grandfather, Abraham. Then, in Genesis 28:15, He said, "I am with you and will watch over you wherever you go, and I will bring you back to this land. I will not leave you until I have done what I have promised you."

Jacob found his way to his mother's family. He stayed with his mother's brother, a conniving cheat named Laban who gave Jacob way more than a taste of his own medicine. Jacob fell in love with the younger of Laban's two daughters. He worked seven years for Rachel's hand in marriage. Then, on what should have been their wedding night, Laban pulled a switch. He slipped his oldest daughter, Leah, into the marriage bed instead. Jacob had a rude awakening next morning, to say the least. When he confronted his uncle, Laban claimed it was local custom that the elder daughter be married first. But once the honeymoon week was over, he'd give Jacob Rachel too—if Jacob labored seven more years as a shepherd for the second wife. What could Jacob do? He agreed.

Years passed. Jacob worked off his debt, but he had other run-ins with his father-in-law. God protected and blessed Jacob through it all. Finally, God told Jacob it was time to return to Canaan. He snuck away with his family and possessions. Laban gave chase, but God brokered a peace—not just between Jacob and Laban, but between Jacob and Esau, the brother who once wanted to kill him.

Jacob wasn't perfect through all of this, but God was faithful to keep His promise and rescue Jacob—even from himself. And when God finally drew Jacob home, He allowed Jacob to wrestle with Him, changed Jacob's name to Israel, and from his descendants birthed the One who would rescue all mankind from our sins—Jesus the Messiah.

Von was Martha's first best pal and protector. Jesus is her Savior and Forever Friend. He has put His Spirit within her to constantly watch over her. And someday, He will take her gently by the sleeve and draw her home to eternity with Him.

> *You are my hiding place;*
> *   you will protect me from trouble*
> *   and surround me with songs of deliverance.*
> *(Psalm 32:7)*

CONSIDER THIS:

Have you ever wandered off, like little Martha, and had God step between you and danger? What happened? How did God protect you? Is there an area of your life right now where you have strayed and God is tugging at your sleeve?

The Dog Who Just Jumped In
Rescue May Get Messy

Rules are not necessarily sacred, principles are.
FRANKLIN D. ROOSEVELT

Sam was a dog who wasn't afraid to get a little messy fulfilling his calling, even if he had to bend a rule in the process. That led to a couple of interesting rescues.

The Lee family adopted Sam when he was a puppy. They had two young daughters and would soon add a third. He was a yellow Labrador retriever, a breed they'd heard was great with kids. Sure enough, Sam quickly decided a big part of his mission in life was to keep "his" children safe.

The oldest daughter, MacKenzie, is in college now, but she will never forget a time when she was nine. All the Lees, including Sam, had gone camping. Kenzie and her five-year-old sister, Kati, wanted to look around a little. This was fine with their parents, with one caution. A river flowed near their campsite. Mom and Dad warned the girls that *they must not jump in, no matter what.*

Kenzie and Kati started off on their adventure. They had each been given a little money in a wallet, and Kati took hers along. The girls wound up at the river. All was well until little Kati dropped her wallet into the water. She was dismayed at the loss and began to cry.

Kenzie decided to save her sister from this minor disaster, ignored her parents' warning, and jumped in to retrieve it.

Kenzie broke a rule—not just the letter of it, but the spirit too. This rule was intended to keep the children safe. Kenzie thought her sister's sobs were a much bigger deal than going in the river, which seemed to her rather shallow at this point. What she didn't realize was that the river bottom dropped off suddenly to a depth of about nine feet. To make matters worse, she had jumped in fully clothed, and her shirt, jeans, and sneakers quickly got waterlogged and began to drag her down. To top it off, she hit a current and could feel the water swirling around her.

Kenzie realized she couldn't get out!

Sam could see his beloved Kenzie was in trouble, so into the river he leaped. He had on a collar and leash. Kenzie grabbed those, and he pulled her back onto the riverbank and out of danger.

Thanks to her dog, Kenzie barely had time to realize she was in trouble before she was rescued from it. I believe Sam was an instrument of God's grace. God saved Kenzie from her poor choice and showed her along the way that when it comes to rivers—and a lot of other things—parents' wisdom is usually greater than that of little girls.

Ah, but is it greater than the wisdom of faithful dogs? Sam apparently didn't think so—at least not when it interfered with another of his rescue missions. That is why he repeatedly bent a certain house rule.

This rule had to do with where Sam could and could not go in the Lee home. Sam was a big dog, and though shorthaired, could shed a substantial amount of fur. Mom and Dad Lee didn't want dog hairs everywhere. They taught Sam he could hang out in the kitchen and laundry room, but the rest of the house was off-limits.

Most of the time, Sam respected this rule. He was a really good dog. But there was one particular situation where he breached his boundaries. He didn't do it on some doggie whim to serve his own purposes. He did it to comfort and protect Kati.

Once a month the entire Lee family drove a few miles to attend a special gathering they all enjoyed. It involved dinner, some worship, and a pastoral message. Kati started taking a dance class that conflicted with this activity. This was years after the river incident, and she was easily old enough to come home and stay by herself for a couple of hours. She would eat dinner and then do homework till the others returned. Kati did her homework in the living room, and even though she was perfectly safe, she felt a little nervous with the rest of her family gone.

Sam picked up on Kati's emotions. On these evenings only, he would go just beyond the edge of the kitchen and lie next to Kati as she sat and studied. She felt calmed and protected by the presence of her dog. And though Sam couldn't say so, he most likely felt he was doing his job…and that mattered more than a few dog hairs in the wrong place. It also mattered more than getting lightly chided by Kati's parents when they came home and found those telltale hairs where they didn't belong. He would act guilty and hangdog when they spoke to him about it, but next month, he would breach the boundary again. He cared about Mom and Dad Lee's approval, but he cared about Kati's comfort more.

You might say that Sam obeyed the spirit of the rule. He didn't get his dog hair all over the house. He just got it in one area—the place he needed to be to make Kati feel safe and protected till her family returned. If rescuing Kati from her fears involved a few frowns from her parents, so be it.

Now and then, I attend the same gathering the Lees do. That's where I heard this story. I also learned that their beloved Sam had just died. He was a wonderful friend and companion and rescuer to his family, and they will miss him greatly.

Judging by their faces when they told the tale, the elder Lees clearly took a benevolent view of Sam's boundary transgressions. I think it warmed their hearts that he protected Kati. They also know their Bible quite well, and so they know there are times when being too slavish to the letter of a rule can not only be overly harsh, it can actually work against God's purposes.

Nowhere is this clearer than in Jesus's dealings with the Pharisees. Okay, so they were purposely trying to use the law to trip Jesus up. Even so, they were a rather legalistic bunch. They had piled a whole load of man-made regulations on top of God's law, and they were more concerned with observing the letter of that law and their added rules than with keeping the spirit of it.

One such rule involved "righteous" people not associating with "sinners." You could say that tax collectors and other sinners were supposed to be confined to the kitchen and laundry room. They were not supposed to get their dog hairs on the righteous and defile them. The Pharisees purported to be shocked when Jesus not only breached this boundary, but actually shared a meal with these folks (Matthew 9:10-11). Eating together was an intimate act in those days. Sharing a meal with sinners was thought to defile you—to get you messy. What was Jesus thinking?

Jesus's response? "It is not the healthy who need a doctor, but the sick. But go and learn what this means: 'I desire mercy, not sacrifice.' For I have not come to call the righteous, but sinners" (Matthew 9:12-13).

Actually *all* of them were sinners, and self-righteous Pharisees were worse off than the rest because they didn't recognize their plight. They thought outward observance could save them. But, on a deeper level, being instruments of God's rescue involves going where the dog hair is. It means getting a little messy, getting a bit of fur in the living room, so to speak, in order to share God's love. Jesus didn't become like the tax collectors and sinners He ate with. He led a perfect, holy life. But He went where the hurting people were because, like Sam, He knew His purpose—to rescue them and give them eternal life.

Maybe all of us need to be a bit more like Sam and Jesus. We need to jump in when we see someone in trouble. We need to distinguish between artificial, man-made boundaries and the deeper intent of God's Word. Only then can we truly fulfill God's calling to be instruments of His rescue to a hurting world.

"Now if a boy can be circumcised on the Sabbath so that the law of Moses may not be broken, why are you angry with me for healing a man's whole body on the Sabbath? Stop judging by mere appearances, but instead judge correctly" (John 7:23-24).

CONSIDER THIS:

Has anyone ever had to get messy to rescue you? What did that say to you about their love for you? About God's love for you? Have you felt God calling you to get messy to help someone else? Did you obey? What was difficult? What was rewarding?

When the Dog Says "Don't"
Saved from What We Don't See

The path is smooth that leadeth on to danger.
WILLIAM SHAKESPEARE

My friend Nancy's older brother might not have lived to see her birth if not for the family dog. Decades later, she is still grateful for the alertness and rapid response of that faithful canine.

Tracy was a toddler at the time. The family lived on a corner, so their home was caught in a cross fire of traffic. The backyard had a gate, but somehow the child must have unlatched it. He wandered out and headed for the street.

That's when Zazerax (Zaz), the family boxer, sprang into action. He clearly sensed that moving cars and unaccompanied toddlers did not a good combination make. He launched a two-pronged rescue effort: he barked and he blocked.

Tracy's mom looked out the window and was stunned to see her little one being nudged back from the street and the cars by faithful Zaz. The dog had placed his body between the child and harm's way. He was trying to herd his young charge back toward the safety of the yard. Zaz was persistent and refused to budge in his purpose. Tracy's grateful mom retrieved her truant...and the story had a happy ending.

Would Tracy have been hurt or killed if Zaz hadn't intervened that day? We will never know, but it's certainly possible. And it's possible my friend SJ could have suffered a similar fate from some hidden dangers in her path—if not for her loving yellow Lab mix, Hendrix.

SJ wasn't a child when she nearly walked into trouble. She was a bright and competent young woman with a place of her own and a busy life. She took reasonable precautions. But on a couple of different occasions, she might have been much the worse for a fun trek if not for her heads-up dog.

In one instance, SJ was out hiking with Hendrix in Princeton, New Jersey. It was hot, and they were in a remote area, surrounded by trees, ferns, and rocks. No one else was around. The path they were walking had mud on the side. All of a sudden, Hendrix yanked hard on his leash, jerking SJ to the left. She was stunned. What had gotten into her dog? She gave Hendrix a "what were you thinking?" look. He just stared back. Then, she glanced around. Coiled on the path, looking somewhat groggy, was a poisonous copperhead snake. Had Hendrix not pulled her aside, she would probably have stepped on the reptile and most likely have been bitten.

On another occasion, SJ and Hendrix were hiking on Georgia's Pine Mountain. The path forked, and SJ went left. There was a ledge she didn't see coming, and there were loose rocks on the path. SJ started sliding on the rocks toward the drop. Hendrix was on an extendable leash. He raced in the other direction, ran out the leash, and held firm to keep SJ from falling. To this day, she doesn't know if she would have gone over the side—and is grateful she didn't find out.

In all three of these situations, a human was headed for trouble and didn't realize the threat that was looming. In all three, a dog sensed danger and acted. Which got me thinking about how God sees when we're headed for danger and how He tries to warn us or head us off.

In Old Testament times, He often used the prophets to do this. Elisha played this role in 2 Kings 6. The king of Aram was at war with Israel, and he had an army to back him up. But though Israel's king couldn't see where the Arameans would be camping, God could, and through Elisha, passed on the intel. Recognizing the worth of his watchdog prophet, the king paid attention. Elisha warned him time and again. The king of Aram was beside himself. Second Kings 6:11-12 tells us what he did next:

> He summoned his officers and demanded of them, "Tell me! Which of us is on the side of the king of Israel?"

> "None of us, my lord the king," said one of his officers, "but Elisha, the prophet who is in Israel, tells the king of Israel the very words you speak in your bedroom."

In the early pages of the New Testament, God used a dream to warn the wise men who had journeyed to find and worship "the one who has been born king of the Jews" (Matthew 2:2). Judah's current ruler, the evil King Herod, had asked them to reveal where the child was. They had no idea this would put the babe at risk. God used the dream to "pull them to the left" to sidestep this poisonous snake of a king who wanted baby Jesus dead. They returned to their homeland by another route and avoided Herod altogether.

These days, God uses His Word and His Spirit to warn us of dangers we might not see. One example from my own life springs to mind. A few years ago, I had planned a vacation hundreds of miles from home. But my mom, who'd been in shaky health, didn't want me to go. I didn't want to believe her days were numbered, but God tugged at my heart, and I listened. I planned a getaway much closer to her, and we had extra time together. Shortly thereafter, she died.

God knows where the dangers are. He knows what will happen in our lives before it does. He knows where our loose rocks and ledges are. He knows what spiritual snakes lie in wait for us. But unlike Zaz with Tracy and Hendrix with SJ, He doesn't always preempt our choices. We may need to respond yes or no to His warnings. And we need to confess our sin so it doesn't cause static in our ability to hear them.

If faithful dogs could do so much to rescue their humans from harm, how much more can a faithful, all-knowing God do? Look to Him and let Him look after you.

"Hear me, my people, and I will warn you—
if you would only listen to me, Israel!"
(Psalm 81:8)

CONSIDER THIS:

Has God ever saved you from danger you didn't see? What happened? What did you learn? Have you ever ignored God's warning and suffered for it? Why did you ignore it? What were the consequences? How are you listening for God's voice in your daily life?

From Felon to Savior
God's Refinement Is Rescue

Patience is bitter, but its fruit is sweet.
ARISTOTLE

Ana never dreamed a dog she nicknamed "Phoebe the felon" would become an instrument of God's rescue. God knew all along. He always does. Okay, so Phoebe wasn't exactly Jean Valjean in *Les Miserables*. But her journey was pretty amazing all the same.

Phoebe was a combo dog—a mix of beagle and Jack Russell terrier. A trainer rescued her as a one-year-old stray. When Ana welcomed her into her family, she already had two other dog "kids," an aging poodle named Tatum and a beagle named Sophie. Ana knew Tatum wasn't long for this world and hoped Phoebe would become Sophie's new best buddy and playmate.

Phoebe took a liking to Sophie, but that same feeling did not extend to the other dogs in the neighborhood. Phoebe adored humans, but canines were a different story. Her attitude was, "This is my 'hood!" That made her tough for Ana to handle. Phoebe would pull on her leash on walks and try to bite other hapless pooches they met along the way. But despite these challenges, Ana refused to throw in the dog bone. She thought to herself, *What if this were my human child?*

Handful though Phoebe was, Ana loved her and would not give up on her.

One year later, Tatum moved on to doggie heaven. Phoebe settled in and got better as more years passed. She made her peace with some of the local dogs and fell in love with a male Pomeranian named Joe-Joe. But she'd go ballistic with new dogs or human males in baggy pants. Since Phoebe had been a stray, neither Ana nor anyone else knew what might have happened in her past to prompt such reactions. Phoebe also seemed to feel that Ana favored Sophie over her. Despite Ana's best efforts, Phoebe still remained something of a troubled child. But she was Ana's troubled child—for better or worse.

Phoebe was also a bit of a thief. Once some friends of Ana's stayed over on their way home from a trip, and they had 12 bags of candy they'd bought for gifts. Though they'd been warned not to leave anything new or interesting around, they'd left an open suitcase on a bed with the candy in it. To Ana's horror, all 12 bags were missing. It turned out Phoebe had buried those bags in the backyard.

In the end Sophie, who was five years older than Phoebe, got sick with cancer. She was fifteen by then. Ana gave her medication to keep her comfortable as long as possible. Phoebe tried to help Sophie too, in her own felon way, by opening the back door so her doggie pal could run outside and dodge being given her pills.

Finally, it was time to put Sophie down. Not long after, Phoebe took ill. It turned out she also had cancer. Still, Ana and Phoebe comforted each other. For the first time it was just the two of them, and they cuddled more. Ana would read in bed with Phoebe and say prayers with her.

Phoebe made it six months—until two days after Christmas. Then Ana knew she needed to do what was best for Phoebe. As she wept, Phoebe licked her tears.

Looking back, Ana realizes that Phoebe played a unique role in her life. God used this problem dog to rescue Ana's heart. Phoebe was a comfort after Sophie died, but it was much more than that. Phoebe was the first challenging dog Ana had had. She taught Ana commitment and patience, and made her stronger and more determined.

Ana never realized, but God knew all along, that those special traits of character were preparing her for a unique ministry. For some time now, she's been involved in a special project with her church. It is something she thought she'd never do—work with juveniles 15–18 years old in a detention camp. When she was first approached about it, she refused to go. But finally, on Good Friday, she tagged along to the facility and interacted with the kids. She's been a regular ever since. She has felt compelled to go because she sensed they needed her, just as Phoebe did.

These teens are from tough environments. About half had gang involvement. But Ana sees through their tough outer shell. She senses that inside, many are just kids who need love. The church team has a service with the kids and goes over Scriptures with them. They preach a lot of forgiveness there. Sometimes kids bring up problems in their lives. Ana recalls how one teen had been having a rough time, and she told him, "Just remember, God doesn't give you more than you can take."

God didn't give the apostle Paul more than he could take, either. And, like Ana, God taught Paul patience in dealing with "problem children." Some of these spiritual problem kids were found in the Corinthian church, and Paul wrote a couple of tough letters to them. Paul's God-given mission was to rescue these young believers from destructive and ungodly attitudes and actions for their own good. We get a glimpse of this in 2 Corinthians 6:4-7,11-13 (CEV):

> But in everything and in every way we show that we truly are God's servants. We have always been patient, though we have had a lot of trouble, suffering, and hard times. We have been beaten, put in jail, and hurt in riots. We have worked hard and have gone without sleep or food. But we have kept ourselves pure and have been understanding, patient, and kind. The Holy Spirit has been with us, and our love has been real. We have spoken the truth, and God's power has worked in us. In all our struggles we have said and done only what is right...

Friends in Corinth, we are telling the truth when we say that there is room in our hearts for you. We are not holding back on our love for you, but you are holding back on your love for us. I speak to you as I would speak to my own children. Please make room in your hearts for us.

Ana loves God. He holds her heart and gives her love and patience to reach out to hurting dogs and humans. He used a four-pawed "felon" to prepare her for even deeper ministry. Is there a "problem" pet or person in your life who might be a tool of God to hone you for deeper service to Him?

Through patience a ruler can be persuaded,
and a gentle tongue can break a bone.
(Proverbs 25:15)

CONSIDER THIS:

How has God been refining you lately? How did it rescue you? How did it equip you to minister to others? Is there a two-footed or four-footed "Phoebe the felon" in your life you need to thank God for?

Chaz in Charge
God Shepherds His Children

*I cannot think of any need in childhood as
strong as the need for a father's protection.*
SIGMUND FREUD

When my cousin Suzanne and her younger brother, Mike, were
kids, they had a wonderful Hungarian vizsla named Chaz. He was 60-
something pounds of close-cropped reddish fur and doggie muscle
with the heart of a loyal, loving, protective shepherd.

That heart was tested and proven in a rather dramatic way when
Suzanne was about 11 years old. Her dad was in the service and the family was living on a military base. Her mom had become friends with a
neighbor woman, and she and her husband came to dinner quite often.
Normally Chaz would jump on the couch to be with the family's guests.
With this couple, he declined to do so. He sat on the ground near the
wife and cozied up to her, but didn't seem to care for the husband. At
the time, no one thought much about it. Later, though, Suzanne would
catch the significance of it all. She would realize Chaz must have sensed
a wolf in sheep's clothing long before his humans discovered the man's
true colors.

As time went on, Suzanne's mom learned that her new friend was a battered wife. The situation was so severe that finally, she and some of the woman's other pals conspired to help her flee. They found an apartment for her off base, where they doubted her husband could find her. And, one fateful day, they moved her out.

The woman's husband left work, went home, and discovered his wife and her possessions gone. He mistakenly thought his missing wife was at Suzanne's mom's house and headed over there to retrieve her.

No adults were around. The kids were home alone with the dog. Suzanne had been told what was happening, and her mom had warned her not to answer the door or let the man in if he showed up. When the doorbell rang and she saw him through the peephole, she did just as she'd been instructed. At first it seemed the fellow would go away. Then he returned and rang the bell again and again, anger boiling and steam rising the longer he was ignored. He screamed that he knew his wife was in there, and he demanded to be let in. He pounded on the door with his fists. He was swearing. He was a spewing volcano about to erupt. He was clearly a threatening wolf—and Chaz went into full protective shepherd mode.

Chaz barked like mad. He ran back and forth between the door and his precious children. Eight-year-old Mike was cowering in the kitchen in a fetal position. Big sister Sue was trying to comfort him and at the same time keep tabs on what the livid would-be intruder was doing. She could see through the kitchen window that he was trying to get into the garage, and she knew some of his wife's things were stored there. This was apt to inflame him further.

What kept Suzanne from losing it was the firm belief that if anyone tried to hurt her or her brother, Chaz would intervene to keep them safe. Still, she was afraid to make a phone call while the fuming husband might see her. He would try to get in for a while, then stop, and then come back and start over. Feeling somewhat protected by Chaz, Suzanne kept comforting little Mike and watching for her chance to call for help. Finally, the fellow was gone long enough that she felt safe in phoning another neighbor who was in the know. That neighbor called the military police, and they picked the man up.

The battered wife got safely away and was able to start a new life.

Suzanne and Mike had no lasting trauma from their scare. But ever afterward, Chaz couldn't tolerate the ringing of a doorbell. It affected him for the rest of his life.

Over a quarter of a century later, Suzanne credits Chaz with rescuing her and Mike in at least two ways. His protective presence bucked her up so she could take care of her younger brother. And she believes it was Chaz's barking that got the angry husband to leave long enough for her to call for assistance.

She has also done some reflecting on Chaz's doggie discernment when it came to people. If Chaz liked people, he would push and lean on them till they gave in and sat down. Then he would climb in their lap. But if he didn't care for them, he would sniff them and walk away. Those who flunked quickly dropped out of the picture in Suzanne's life. Those who passed the "Chaz test" usually hung around. In particular, Chaz went nuts for one young boy when Suzanne was 16—and he is now her husband and the father of her own two young children.

If Chaz had lived in another time and place, I think he would have made an excellent sheep dog. He had the heart to rescue his flock and he sensed who might be a threat. And Scripture tells us that our Good Shepherd, Jesus, guards us from the spiritual wolves who seek to attack us.

In John 10:11-12, Jesus says, "I am the good shepherd. The good shepherd lays down his life for the sheep. The hired hand is not the shepherd and does not own the sheep. So when he sees the wolf coming, he abandons the sheep and runs away. Then the wolf attacks the flock and scatters it." Later in the same chapter, in verses 27-30, Jesus adds, "My sheep listen to my voice; I know them, and they follow me. I give them eternal life, and they shall never perish; no one will snatch them out of my hand. My Father, who has given them to me, is greater than all; no one can snatch them out of my Father's hand. I and the Father are one."

As great a heart as Chaz had, as willing as he was to give himself for his people, he was not an all-powerful "shepherd." He could not rescue always or forever. Our Good Shepherd has no such limitations. He offers eternal spiritual rescue to all who trust in Him. Are you safely in His hand, where the wolves can't go?

Who shall separate us from the love of Christ? Shall trouble or hardship or persecution or famine or nakedness or danger or sword? As it is written:

> *"For your sake we face death all day long;*
> *we are considered as sheep to be slaughtered."*

No, in all these things we are more than conquerors through him who loved us. For I am convinced that neither death nor life, neither angels nor demons, neither the present nor the future, nor any powers, neither height nor depth, nor anything else in all creation, will be able to separate us from the love of God that is in Christ Jesus our Lord (Romans 8:35-39).

CONSIDER THIS:

What is the greatest physical danger you've ever been rescued from? Who saved you? How? What impact did it have? What is the greatest spiritual danger you've ever faced? Who did you turn to? What happened? Have you ever put your faith in Jesus as your Good Shepherd who died to pay for your sins and keep you safe forever?

Part III

Four-Foots Lifting Four-Foots

🐾 Caleb and Louie Belle 🐾

Fee! Fie! Foe! Fam!

From Predator to Protector

The important thing is this: to be ready at any moment
to sacrifice what you are for what you could become.
AUTHOR UNKNOWN

Do you know where the title of this story comes from? It's the somewhat altered first line of a certain famous ogre's perverse verse from the fairy tale *Jack and the Beanstalk*. The full rhyme goes this way:

> Fee-fie-fo-fum!
> I smell the blood of an Englishman.
> Be he 'live or be he dead,
> I'll grind his bones to make my bread!

No self-respecting fairy tale Jack would entrust himself to an ogre like that, much less expect that ogre to turn into his rescuer, would he? So why would anyone think a cat named Louie Belle could entrust herself to a Korean jindo named Caleb, whose breed has an extremely strong prey drive?

Because truth can be way stranger than fiction, especially when God is involved.

Caleb and Louie Belle share a pair of humans—my friend Pamela and her husband, Jay. Louie Belle got there first. Caleb entered the picture as a seven-month-old rescue Pamela thought would be only a temporary addition. God had other plans. Pamela has some serious health issues, one of which used to cause her to collapse without warning. I've written elsewhere in this book about how Caleb began to spontaneously alert her when this was about to happen, and she recognized her new dog was God's provision for her.

Still, Pamela and Jay were warned that Louie Belle could be at risk from Caleb. Jindos have been known to kill small pets, including cats, and sometimes eat them. Louie Belle, a rescue too, had come to Pamela and Jay declawed. If Caleb's hunting instincts took over, she didn't have any way to defend herself. She'd already been attacked by vicious stray cats who'd come into their yard. Against a dog of Caleb's size and strength, she'd be even more helpless.

Pamela was determined that if Caleb ever went after Louie Belle, they would need to re-home him. She didn't want to chance that possibility. For this reason, Caleb was never allowed to be loose around the cat. Inside, he was either in a locked kennel or on a leash attached to Pamela. Outside, he was on a zip line so he couldn't get near Louie Belle if she came through the cat door into the backyard.

Caleb proved the wisdom of his master's precautions the first few days the cat was in his sights. He fixed her with his "hunter's stare." He slammed himself against his kennel. Outside, he lunged, but the zip line was plenty strong and held.

For her part, Louie Belle was terrified of the new dog in her world, but in time, she learned he couldn't get to her.

Though restraining Caleb was a temporary solution, it was not a desirable long-term fix. Pamela wanted to transform Caleb from the cat's foe to her family. She decided to try an alpha dog approach with Caleb. Dogs are pack animals. The alpha is the pack leader, and it doesn't always need to be a dog. Dogs can perceive their human masters as their alphas if they're trained to do so. Pamela's strategy was to try to get Caleb to perceive Louie Belle as ranking higher in the pack than he—even of being his alpha. She had several ways of trying to get this message across.

Since the alpha gets everything first—because the alpha ensures the pack's survival—Pamela put Louie Belle's hairs on all of Caleb's stuff. That included his bed, his toys, and even a few in his food. She let a leashed Caleb watch her offer his food to the kitty. Only after Louie Belle turned up her nose at it did he get fed. Pamela put Louie Belle on top of Caleb's kennel and made him lie down in it in submission. When Louie Belle walked into a room, Pamela and Jay stopped everything to pay attention to her, their little alpha queen.

Caleb got the message. Before his humans could even prompt him, he stopped giving Louie Belle his hunter stare. Instead, when she entered his presence, he looked at the ceiling. After all, you can't hunt your alpha, right?

This was encouraging. It got more so. Under the ever-present and watchful eyes of their human masters, Louie Belle and Caleb slowly got to be buddies. They went from sniffing each other to taking naps together. If Louie Belle approached Caleb when he was eating, he backed off to let his alpha have first dibs on his food. Still, Pamela could not be certain if Caleb was doing this only to please her. Would he act differently if she weren't there? She didn't dare leave the two alone together—at least not yet.

Three months passed. One night Jay took Caleb for a walk. Louie Belle was ticked. Her life revolved around Jay, and her special human was paying attention to the dog. She went from window to window, mewing. She wouldn't let Pamela hold her. It was Jay she wanted.

When Jay returned, Pamela told him he'd better go make nice to Louie Belle. He sat with her on the hearth while she let him know her hurt feelings. Caleb jumped up on the sofa next to Pamela, his human alpha. When she gave him a dog biscuit, he laid it in front of her to be sure she didn't want a bite first.

Meanwhile, Louie Belle was still expressing her displeasure to Jay. Caleb took in the situation. Finally, he mouthed his dog biscuit, plopped it down in front of Louie Belle, and jumped back on the sofa, tail wagging happily, thoroughly pleased with himself for making everything all better.

"Jay, I can't believe what I just saw," Pamela said. "I've never seen a dog give another dog his treat, let alone a dog give a cat his treat!" Jay was stunned too. Louie Belle was simply disgusted. Why would any self-respecting feline want a peanut-butter-flavored biscuit with dog slobber on it? She stalked away, leaving the treat untouched.

From that moment, Pamela knew that Louie Belle was safe with Caleb. He knew Louie Belle's place in the pack and his heart was to care for the kitty. Pamela was right. Caleb became Louie Belle's protector. She went outside only with him. The vicious stray cats got the picture too. They realized Louie Belle had a rescuer in Caleb and quit coming around. That meant Louie Belle stopped getting cat bites that resulted in costly vet visits.

So, what transformed Caleb from this cat's potential predator to her protector and rescuer? His human masters changed his perception of her.

In a sense, you could say the same thing happened to the apostle Paul.

Paul started life as Saul of Tarsus. He was a devout Jew who studied with the finest religious teachers of his day. He became a Pharisee of the Pharisees whose greatest desire was to please and serve his "Alpha," God. He thought one way to do this was to hunt apostates. First on his list was a new sect called the Way who believed that Jesus of Nazareth was the promised Messiah and God incarnate.

Saul was present when Stephen was stoned, and Acts 8:1 tells us that Saul "approved of their killing him." In Acts 9:1-2, things escalate even further. "Saul was still breathing out murderous threats against the Lord's disciples. He went to the high priest and asked him for letters to the synagogues in Damascus, so that if he found any there who belonged to the Way, whether men or women, he might take them as prisoners to Jerusalem."

Saul headed for Damascus in full hunter mode. Then he had an unexpected encounter with his Alpha. A blinding light flashed. "He fell to the ground and heard a voice say to him, 'Saul, Saul, why do you persecute me?'" (Acts 9:4).

Saul asked who it was. It was Jesus. Saul was told to get up, go into

Damascus, and wait for instructions from his Alpha. But he had to be led there. He'd been struck blind.

Now the Lord told a believer named Ananias to go to Saul. Ananias wasn't thrilled with his assignment. Wasn't Saul a hunter of Christians? If he wasn't in a crate or on a zip line, how could Ananias possibly be safe in his presence?

He could be safe because the Alpha of alphas, God Himself, was turning Saul's perceptions on their ear and rescuing Saul from himself. In Acts 9:15-16 we read, "But the Lord said to Ananias, 'Go! This man is my chosen instrument to proclaim my name to the Gentiles and their kings and to the people of Israel. I will show him how much he must suffer for my name.'"

Ananias obeyed. Saul got his physical sight back—and his spiritual sight as well. He became Paul, and spent the rest of his life as an instrument of God's rescue, bringing both Jews and Gentiles to faith in Jesus. He was beaten, shipwrecked, imprisoned, and eventually gave his life for his faith. But he never stopped serving the Lord and His church.

Louie Belle was safe with Caleb because Pamela and Jay transformed him. But, in a deeper sense, God did. He had a purpose for Caleb being in this family. He also had a mission for Paul, and transformed him into one who loved and nurtured believers, even at the cost of his life.

We are all like Caleb and Paul. We need to be saved from ourselves so God can use us with others. We need this not only in a once-and-for-all way, but in smaller, ongoing ways all through our lives. Will you allow Him to transform you so that you might be not foe but family to those He longs to entrust to your care?

I was personally unknown to the churches of Judea that are in Christ. They only heard the report: "The man who formerly persecuted us is now preaching the faith he once

tried to destroy." And they praised God because of me (Galatians 1:22-24).

CONSIDER THIS:

How has God rescued you from yourself? How has that helped you reach out to others? Has He ever transformed you from "foe" to "family" in someone's life? What happened? How has that changed your perceptions in an ongoing way?

His Paw Was on the Sparrow
God Cares for the Least of Us

*A real friend is one who walks in when
the rest of the world walks out.*
WALTER WINCHELL

Hendrix was a very large dog with a huge heart for those in need. That included some rather tiny members of God's creation. His doting human mom, SJ, told me her yellow Labrador retriever mix tried to rescue anyone around him who needed it.

One tiny being Hendrix saved became the dog's lifelong friend. Hendrix was with SJ on vacation and they were hiking together. Hendrix heard something. The big guy darted his head, blinked, sniffed the air, and headed for a bush. When he returned, he had two bits of fluff hanging out of the sides of his mouth. SJ started to scold him…till he spat out a tiny kitten covered in dog slobber. Hendrix licked the itsy-bitsy baby from rear end to face with one giant swipe of his tongue. He hadn't meant the kitty any harm—he was trying to help.

SJ put the female kitten in a box and took her home. She named the orphan Lenie after a high-school friend. Lenie thought Hendrix was her mom. He'd put his tongue down like a ladder, she'd crawl up it, and he'd ferry her around in his open mouth. When she got too big for that, he'd carry her like a mama cat does her young.

Hendrix also bathed Lenie and taught her to eat. SJ put the kitty's formula in a saucer. Hendrix set Lenie on the saucer and she ate spread-eagled, copying him as he gobbled his dog chow.

Lenie thought she was a dog. She went with Hendrix and SJ to the park and the beach. Hendrix taught her to hike and to swim. She'd stand on the seashore and squeal. Hendrix would pick her up, paddle out about ten feet, and put her in the water. She'd swim to shore, and he'd swim beside her and watch her the whole time to make certain she was safe.

Hendrix also sprang to the aid of other small critters in need—even if it meant challenging a friend. At one point, he and SJ had a black chow for a neighbor. Her name was Chowder, and she had a hunting instinct. One day Hendrix came upon her with a groundhog in her mouth. Chowder was about to shake the hapless creature, but Hendrix rushed her and plowed into her. Chowder dropped her prey, stunned. Hendrix pinned her and held her at bay until the groundhog escaped.

Then there was the day Hendrix found a ferret in the snow. SJ figured it was someone's escaped pet. She took it home and put it in a crate with some food. But the ferret just cried and shivered. Later she discovered the foundling sleeping on Hendrix's belly, warmed by the dog's body heat. Hendrix cared for the ferret for eleven days—till SJ found its owner.

When I think of Hendrix's rescue and tender care of creatures he could have squashed with his paw, it makes me smile and think of our Lord. The prophet Isaiah's description of Messiah gives us a peek into how He views the small and struggling of this world:

> "Take a good look at my servant.
>   I'm backing him to the hilt.
> He's the one I chose,
>   and I couldn't be more pleased with him...
> He won't brush aside the bruised and the hurt
>   and he won't disregard the small and insignificant,
>   but he'll steadily and firmly set things right."
>   (Isaiah 42:1,3 MSG)

God's heart is for us to be His arms and legs in this rescue effort, as Matthew 25 confirms. Jesus is talking about the Second Coming. He describes how the Son of Man will separate the sheep from the goats.

> "He will put the sheep on his right and the goats on his left.

> "Then the King will say to those on his right, 'Come, you who are blessed by my Father; take your inheritance, the kingdom prepared for you since the creation of the world. For I was hungry and you gave me something to eat, I was thirsty and you gave me something to drink, I was a stranger and you invited me in, I needed clothes and you clothed me, I was sick and you looked after me, I was in prison and you came to visit me.'

> "Then the righteous will answer him, 'Lord, when did we see you hungry and feed you, or thirsty and give you something to drink? When did we see you a stranger and invite you in, or needing clothes and clothe you? When did we see you sick or in prison and go to visit you?'

> "The King will reply, 'Truly I tell you, whatever you did for one of the least of these brothers and sisters of mine, you did for me'" (Matthew 25:33-40).

Hendrix was a dog after God's own heart. He set a shining example we humans would do well to follow. No creature was too weak or small to be ignored by this big-hearted canine. If he saw a need, he reached out and met it in whatever way he could. And when he recently passed from this world, one of those who stayed by him to comfort him in his last days was the tiny kitten he had saved all those years before.

Are there people or animals in your life God is nudging you to reach out to, small and seemingly insignificant though they may be? If you take a page from Hendrix and care about and for them, who knows how you may be blessed in return?

"'When you reap the harvest of your land, do not reap to the very edges of your field or gather the gleanings of your harvest. Leave them for the poor and for the foreigner residing among you. I am the Lord *your God'" (Leviticus 23:22).*

CONSIDER THIS:

Have you ever been needy and hurting or felt small and weak and had someone reach out to you? What happened? How did it affect your life? How did it affect your relationship with the Lord? How might God want you to do this for others?

Dog, Hamster, and King
God's Rescue Ways Aren't Ours

Human salvation demands the divine disclosure of truths surpassing reason.

Thomas Aquinas

Nikki the Siberian husky didn't have a heart for helping hamsters. He was much more likely to eat one than save one. But on this particular day, his human master, Don, didn't have any other handy options for "search and rescue."

It was summer, and Don and his dog were about to fly from California to join the rest of the family at their vacation home in Maine. It was an annual pilgrimage away from busy lives and ringing phones to rest, relaxation, and much-needed family bonding. But there was an unexpected glitch in Don's well-oiled getaway machinery. The family hamster was missing.

This tiny truant had put its person in a big mess. Don had planned to leave the hamster with a friend. If he flew away without locating it, the hamster would probably be dead of dehydration before the family returned. Clearly the hamster was in big trouble, though it was blithely unaware of this fact. Which left Don with the prospect of missing his nonrefundable flight—or convincing the airline that coming to the aid of a hamster in distress was worthy of a free rebook. Yeah, right.

Fortunately, Don thought of one other, unconventional option. Nikki was always nosing around for the hamster. Maybe, under his watchful eye, his dog could be the unwitting instrument of its salvation.

Don turned Nikki loose in his daughter Anna's room, where the hamster had last been seen. Nikki sniffed around, then stuck his nose in a boot. Don pulled the boot off his dog's snout, turned it upside down, and voila! One missing hamster found. Don got the hamster delivered, and he and Nikki got to the airport in time to make the plane.

Talk about a creative way to get out of a pickle. It didn't matter that Nikki could probably have crushed that hamster with one paw. He was not the superior intelligence here. Don was.

And as brilliant as Nebuchadnezzar was, he was not the superior intelligence in ancient Babylon. God was.

King Nebuchadnezzar was the most powerful ruler and conqueror of his day. When he went sniffing out other kingdoms, it surely wasn't to make nice. But God's people in the kingdom of Judah were suffering from spiritual dehydration and were not allowing His prophets to "find" them. They refused to face the danger their idolatry put them in, persecuting God's messengers instead. Drastic measures were called for. God allowed this pagan ruler to conquer His people and transplant a huge number of them to Babylon and its surroundings.

But, you say, that wasn't rescue. That was judgment. Yes, but it was rescue too. It helped at least some Israelites rethink their spiritual loyalties and fall on their knees before the Lord. It also brought a witness of Him to the peoples among whom the Jews were resettled—and a prophet named Daniel into Nebuchadnezzar's own court. What's more, God had placed His people in a "boot" that offered His protection and promised restoration.

We see huge glimpses of that boot in action in the book of Daniel. Daniel and three of his godly friends honored God with their food choices and survived and thrived on vegetables in the king's court. Daniel saved himself and his fellow court wise men from execution by correctly interpreting Nebuchadnezzar's dream—courtesy of divine revelation. His three friends Shadrach, Meshach, and Abednego emerged unharmed from a fiery furnace where they'd been cast for refusing to worship a gold statue. And God used Daniel to even more dramatically get Nebuchadnezzar's attention. He had Daniel interpret yet another dream, warning the king he'd be judged for his pride and literally put out to pasture, thinking and acting like an animal. When Nebuchadnezzar failed to make an attitude adjustment, the prophecy came to pass. Nebuchadnezzar came to his senses only when he acknowledged God's sovereignty. Some think he also came to saving faith. Whether or not that happened, he most definitely made the Jews' worship of the Lord politically correct.

Nebuchadnezzar died before the 70 years of captivity were up. Daniel survived him to continue his worship and witness. As an old man he showed off God's "boot" once again, to King Darius, by emerging unscathed from the lions' den he'd been thrown into for praying to God. And when the 70 years were up, God kept His promise and delivered a remnant of His people back to their land, where they rebuilt Jerusalem and His temple.

So, what does all this mean for you and me right now? For me, it means God is sovereign over *everything*. He's at work to rescue even when I don't know I'm in trouble. And when I do—when I'm feeling like a tiny lost hamster—God knows where I am. Even if I feel like He's jumped on a plane to Maine and left me, I know that's not true because His Word says He will never forsake His children. Even if His means of rescue seems like it will destroy me—like Nikki with the hamster and Nebuchadnezzar with the Israelites—I know He's got me in His boot, and always will.

> *"Hear the word of the LORD, you nations;*
> *proclaim it in distant coastlands:*
> *'He who scattered Israel will gather them*
> *and will watch over his flock like a shepherd.'*

> For the LORD will deliver Jacob
>   and redeem them from the hand of those stronger
>   than they."
>
>   (Jeremiah 31:10-11)

CONSIDER THIS:

When was the last time you felt small, lost, or helpless? Who or what did you turn to? What happened? Has God ever used what seemed like destruction to rescue you? How has this affected your perception of Him?

Sultan's Heavy Lifting
Prayer Triggers Rescue

Prayer is the greatest of all forces, because it honors God and brings Him into active aid.
E.M. BOUNDS

Once upon a time and not too very long ago, Martha had a horse she jumped and showed. It was stabled near her L.A. home. A trainer there had a Jack Russell terrier who seemed to think he was lord of the barn— or at least barn manager for his master's horses.

This dog, who we'll call Sultan, wanted his barn aisle to run smoothly. Everything had to be in its place. If humans left things lying around in the tack room, this four-footed neatnik would drag the offending items to the trash.

Our take-charge canine also liked symmetry among the horses. Stalls in this barn aisle had two-piece Dutch doors. When the top half was open, a horse might poke its head over the side. Sultan was fine if *all* the horses poked their heads out. He was fine if *none* did. But, if it was a mix, he was one unhappy dog. And he had his ways of persuading his equine charges to see things his way and toe the line.

Such self-appointed watchdog behavior on Sultan's part was merely humorous. But he assigned himself another, much more vital task.

There were times when horses got cast in their stalls, and he would sound an alert.

Casting refers to a situation where a horse can't get up from the ground, which can happen in various ways. At Martha's barn, the soil was sandy. If a horse dug—as some will do—it could create a gap between the bottom of the wood stall and the ground beneath. This could lead to a scenario in which a horse was down with its foot stuck in that hole, unable to rise.

We humans love to get horizontal. It helps us relax and recharge. But horses are built to sleep standing up. If they are down too long, they can actually suffocate from their digestive system pressing on their lungs. They may also panic and injure themselves or others with their thrashing, flailing attempts to get back on their feet. And if a horse rolled in its stall and got a leg caught, it could rip that leg up pretty badly struggling to get free.

Sultan didn't have the strength, skill, or smarts to help a cast horse or even understand the situation. But he did understand when a horse was in trouble. He would start barking and *keep on barking* until his master showed up to come to that horse's aid.

Sultan instinctively barked for his master to come to the rescue. God wants us to do the same. He wants us to be alert to spot those in distress and cry out to Him for help on their behalf.

A wonderful example of this is the story of the Canaanite woman in Matthew 15:21-28. This woman's daughter was in terrible trouble. She was demon-possessed, and the mom had no idea how to free her child from this horrible bondage. But she believed that Jesus could help. She went to Him and pleaded for rescue. And when at first He didn't reply, she kept right on "barking."

Jesus's disciples got annoyed and asked Him to tell her to leave. He told the woman, "I was sent only to the lost sheep of Israel" (15:24). That did not shut this mother up. She got on her knees and begged. Then He told her, "It is not right to take the children's bread and toss it to the dogs" (15:26). But she was tenacious and she had an answer. "Even the dogs eat the crumbs that fall from their master's table" (15:27).

Jesus acknowledged her "great faith" and gave her the rescue she wanted.

So, what does a barking dog in a barn have in common with a first-century Canaanite mama and us today? I think there are some common threads that can teach us a great deal about God's rescue and what part we may play in it.

First, both the dog and the Canaanite woman recognized there was a problem. They realized another living being needed help. How often do we walk through our world without really picking up on a person's or animal's distress even though it is right in front of us?

Second, they realized on some level that the problem was beyond them. Dogs like Sultan weigh an average of 14 to 18 pounds. Horses in Martha's barn were typically 1800 to 2000 pounds—at least a hundred times Sultan's weight. No way could that dog do such heavy lifting. Nor was Sultan possessed of a human's advanced thought processes to figure out how to help such an animal cooperate in the rescue effort. He was way over his doggie head…and somehow had enough horse sense to know it.

The Canaanite mom also recognized that she was way out of her depth. But we humans aren't always this savvy. We may neglect to "bark" for our Master and seek His wisdom, power, and provision… attempting to handle things in our own puny strength instead. But if we are willing to seek God, He will help us even with our prayers. According to Romans 8:26-27 (NASB), "In the same way the Spirit also helps our weakness; for we do not know how to pray as we should, but the Spirit Himself intercedes for us with groanings too deep for words; and He who searches the hearts knows what the mind of the Spirit is, because He intercedes for the saints according to the will of God."

Third, both Sultan and the Canaanite woman were tenacious in pleading for rescue. Neither quit "barking" until they got the help they sought. Jesus advocated persistence in prayer and even told His disciples a parable about it (Luke 18:1-8). I have a friend who prayed 15 years before her niece came to know the Lord. That niece is now a joyful daughter of the King.

There is another extremely significant element both situations share. In both cases, the ones needing help also needed assistance drawing attention to their plight. Without the barking of a watchdog, things might well have ended badly. Nor would it have helped to bark to just anyone. Only the master had the knowledge and power that was needed.

If you are God's child, He is calling you to be a watchdog too. He wants you to stay alert for those who need His rescue. He desires that you bark persistently to Him on their behalf. And as you bless others with your prayers and see God's answers in their lives, your own faith will grow.

I've posted watchmen on your walls, Jerusalem.
Day and night they keep at it, praying, calling out,
reminding GOD to remember.
They are to give him no peace until he does what he said,
until he makes Jerusalem famous as the City of Praise.
(Isaiah 62:6-7 MSG)

CONSIDER THIS:

When was the last time God answered your prayers for someone who was down and stuck? What happened? How did it affect the one you prayed for? How did it impact your own relationship with God? How is God calling you to persevere in prayer right now?

Half-Pound Savior
The Small Can Stand Tall

Even the smallest person can change
the course of the future.
J.R.R. Tolkien, *The Lord of the Rings*

When tiny Mica was born by C-section on December 7, 2011, she seemed like the last dog on the planet who could rescue anyone. Indeed, she desperately needed rescuing herself. This tiny puppy was the runt of her litter and weighed only 2.21 ounces. Her two brothers, each double her birth weight, were pushing her out of the way when they nursed. It was touch and go whether she would even survive.

I read the news of Mica's birth over dinner in Southern California, across the country from where she was fighting to live. I had hoped for a female puppy from this litter, and she was the only girl. Amazingly, she had been born on what would have been my father's one hundredth birthday. But she was miniscule even given her tiny parents, a purebred toy sheltie and a poshie (Pomeranian/toy sheltie mix). I knew it was out of my hands. I put her in God's hands and prayed.

Over the next five days, Miracle Mica doubled her birth weight. Even her vet was amazed. Granted, her human "mom," my dear friend Charlotte, tube fed the puppy. But tube feeding doesn't always save such tiny ones, and it certainly doesn't always have such dramatically quick results.

Little did I know that even more dramatic results were to follow.

One of Charlotte's other dogs was a toy Australian shepherd who'd had multiple homes and needed TLC. Doodle Bug had come to live with Charlotte just the month before. Doodle loved her new family, and it turned out that Doodle was also bringing a family with her. Ten days after Mica was born, Doodle gave birth, also by C-section, to four tiny puppies of her own.

Doodle's milk had come in early, and she was also naturally well-endowed. The result was not ideal. Her "equipment" was engorged, and her tiny puppies were having a struggle getting their teensy mouths around their mom's nursers. They were also fighting Charlotte's efforts to tube feed them.

Charlotte was keeping her friends apprised on Facebook of the puppy crisis. I recalled that human moms expressed their milk so others could feed their babies when they had to be gone for a few hours. I messaged Charlotte. Could this kind of thing be done for Doodle?

Not exactly, but Charlotte got another idea. Mica was now almost two weeks old and nearly half a pound. She was significantly larger than Doodle's puppies, but still a runt herself. Extra milk could only help her, right? And putting Mica on Doodle might relieve Doodle's engorgement and make it easier for her own puppies to nurse.

Mica performed her rescue mission happily and quickly. She weighed over an ounce more afterward. After a few hours' break, Mica did her rescue duty once again. It took more time and additional measures, but within a few days, Doodle's puppies were nursing on her and thriving.

It tickled me that my not-yet-two-week-old puppy had been used to help save others. It also reminded me of an overriding truth. When God rescues, He often uses the weak, the "foolish," and the tiny—just to make it abundantly clear that He is the real Rescuer.

Scripture is filled with examples of this, but the one that jumps out at me is the Old Testament story of Gideon. The Israelites had fallen on hard times in Canaan. They had turned to worshipping idols, so

God allowed the Midianites to harass and oppress them, ravaging their crops and livestock.

I love how *The Message* describes what Israel did, and what followed. In Judges 6:6 it says, "The People of Israel, reduced to grinding poverty by Midian, cried out to GOD for help."

In response, the angel of God appeared to a man named Gideon and told him he'd been chosen to save his people. Gideon didn't exactly embrace his mission. His answer was, "*Me*, my master? How and with what could I ever save Israel? Look at me. My clan's the weakest in Manasseh and I'm the runt of the litter" (Judges 6:15 MSG).

God said being the runt didn't matter. He, God, was with Gideon. He, God, would make it happen. Gideon asked for a sign to prove this was true.

In the end, it was actually *two* signs. Judges 6:36-40 (MSG) tells the story:

> Gideon said to God, "If this is right, if you are using me to save Israel as you've said, then look: I'm placing a fleece of wool on the threshing floor. If dew is on the fleece only, but the floor is dry, then I know that you will use me to save Israel, as you said."

> That's what happened. When he got up early the next morning, he wrung out the fleece—enough dew to fill a bowl with water!

> Then Gideon said to God, "Don't be impatient with me, but let me say one more thing. I want to try another time with the fleece. But this time let the fleece stay dry, while the dew drenches the ground."

> God made it happen that very night. Only the fleece was dry while the ground was wet with dew.

Gideon got on board with God's plan. He led an army of men to do battle with the Midianites. But now God started making adjustments. Gideon's army was too large. God wanted it to be much, much smaller so that the Israelites would have to recognize that they'd been saved by God's strength, not their own.

God ordered Gideon to tell his men that anyone who was afraid or had qualms could leave. Twenty-two companies of warriors bailed. That left ten companies—still too many for God's liking. He had Gideon take his men down to a stream to drink. God told Gideon to keep those who lapped water with their tongues and send the rest home.

That cut Gideon down to 300 men—against a Midianite force that looked like a swarm of locusts. But, in God's strength and power, this small army stood tall. God gave them the victory, and for the next 40 years, Israel had peace.

Mica and Gideon are visible demonstrations of how God can—and does—use anyone or anything to rescue. It's not about us. It's about Him. That's one reason I chose the name Mica for my puppy, a name that means, "Who resembles God?"

Who, indeed? God, the mightiest Being in the universe, who made it all, counts no one out. He counts no one as insignificant to Him. Each of us can make a difference if we look to the Lord and His strength not ours, follow where He leads, and embrace the adventures He offers.

But God chose the foolish things of the world to shame the wise; God chose the weak things of the world to shame the strong. God chose the lowly things of this world and the despised things—and the things that are not—to nullify the things that are, so that no one may boast before him (1 Corinthians 1:27-29).

CONSIDER THIS:

When was the last time you rescued someone? Did you do it in your own strength or God's? What was the result? How has your sense of your own adequacy affected your response to God's calls? How has this impacted your life?

The Litter that Lived
Love Breaches Boundaries

I have come to realize more and more that the greatest disease and the greatest suffering is to be unwanted, unloved, uncared for, to be shunned by everybody, to be just nobody (to no one).
MOTHER TERESA OF CALCUTTA

My new friend Nancy grew up with a mother who was a great animal lover. They had not only cats and dogs, but bunnies, chickens, birds, and hamsters as well. And when a sick, shy, ginger-colored little Pomeranian boy dog showed up at their door, this big-hearted woman coaxed him in and took him under her wing.

It took Nancy's mother six months to treat the little guy's mange and to restore his beautiful long-haired coat. She overcame his shyness to the point where he walked around the table on his hind legs begging with his forefeet. She became quite close to the little fellow. Then, the following winter, the dog got loose on the coldest night. Nancy's mother placed an ad, hoping someone had found him. Someone had. He was returned, but not long after that, he caught the distemper virus and died.

A few weeks after losing her boy, Nancy's mother got a call from the folks who had returned her little truant. He had apparently had his way with their female fox terrier. There was a litter. Would she take a puppy?

How could Nancy's mother resist? She said yes. Nancy thinks there may have been a waiting period because of the distemper virus. When it was over, they welcomed a little female puppy into their home. She had short hair like her mother, but her color came from her father, and they named her Ginger for that color.

Ginger was a wonderful dog, and she had a great life with her new family. But she never had her own puppies, even though she wasn't spayed. Little did her humans know that Ginger's mommy instincts would be satisfied in a very different and heart-tugging way.

Ginger's turn at motherhood began when the family cat got hit and killed by a car. This cat had a three-week-old litter of kittens. Nancy's family bottle-fed the babies, but who would do all the other vital things a mother does?

Who else but Ginger?

Sweet little Ginger embraced her new charges. She didn't care if they were kitties. They were orphan babies who needed her attention. She was not a respecter of species, and this cross-cultural adoption didn't faze her in the least. She licked those kittens. She loved on them. She let them crawl all over her. She let them nurse on her, even though she had no milk. She stayed right by their side, gave them warmth and comfort, and never left them. Every single kitten lived. When they were old enough, Nancy's mom found homes for them all.

Ginger probably understood a few simple verbal commands from her masters. But she didn't know what God says about caring for orphans. She just followed her doggie instincts and compassionate nature.

The most famous biblical cross-cultural adoptive mom likely did much the same thing when she scooped baby Moses out of the Nile.

Actually, at that point, poor little Moses didn't even have a name yet. What he *did* have was a life-threatening problem. He was a Hebrew male infant in Egypt, and Pharaoh had ordered all Hebrew baby boys thrown into the Nile to die.

Moses's birth mother couldn't save him—not that she didn't try. She hid him for three whole months. When she realized she couldn't conceal him any longer, she put him in a waterproofed basket and set it among the reeds in the river. Moses's older sister hid nearby and watched to see what would take place.

What happened was a God-orchestrated cross-cultural rescue. Pharaoh's daughter showed up with some of her maidens. She'd come to bathe in the river. She saw the basket and had one of her maidens go get it and bring it to her. According to Exodus 2:6-10 (MSG),

> She opened it and saw the child—a baby crying! Her heart went out to him. She said, "This must be one of the Hebrew babies."
>
> Then his sister was before her: "Do you want me to go and get a nursing mother from the Hebrews so she can nurse the baby for you?"
>
> Pharaoh's daughter said, "Yes. Go." The girl went and called the child's mother.
>
> Pharaoh's daughter told her, "Take this baby and nurse him for me. I'll pay you." The woman took the child and nursed him.
>
> After the child was weaned, she presented him to Pharaoh's daughter who adopted him as her son. She named him Moses (Pulled-Out), saying, "I pulled him out of the water."

I doubt Pharaoh's daughter knew much, if anything, about the God of the Hebrews. She likely didn't rescue Moses for biblical reasons. Whether or not she was a birth mom at this point, she seemed to have the instincts of a mother. She felt a tug of compassion. And, of course, God wanted this baby rescued for His sovereign purposes.

Decades later, at about age 80, God used Moses to rescue an entire nation. In God's power, Moses pulled the Hebrews out of Egypt. The Red Sea parted to let them through and then closed its waters to drown the pursuing Egyptian army. If that seems a poor repayment for the rescue of Moses, consider this. Through that nation, centuries later, would come a baby, Jesus of Nazareth, who was Messiah and would die to save *all* people from their sins.

Ginger adopted a litter of kittens. Pharaoh's daughter adopted one Hebrew baby boy. But God is the consummate cross-cultural Adopter. He is not a respecter of persons. He loves each and every one of us as if there were no other. He invites us to join His family, nurse on His Word, and be cared for and loved by Him forever! Will you let Him draw you close?

He doesn't care how great a person may be,
  and he pays no more attention to the rich than to
    the poor.
He made them all.
                    (Job 34:19 NLT)

CONSIDER THIS:

Have you ever been rescued or cared for by someone outside your family and cultural context? Did it surprise you? Did it bless you? How did it change your perception of people and God? Is God calling you to reach across some artificial human boundary to love others in His name right now?

The Shelter Evac Built

God Spotlights Needs

The heart has eyes which the brain knows nothing of.
CHARLES HENRY PARKHURST

When New Orleans, Louisiana, was slammed by Hurricane Katrina, not just people but animals were in dire straits. In the midst of that swirling crisis, one half-drowned dog became a lifeline—just by virtue of being in the wrong place at the right time.

In the course of that awful storm, the New Orleans jail was flooded. Seven thousand inmates had to be removed. They were taken to the top of the interstate, put in buses under armed guard, and transported to various facilities throughout the state, including Dixon Correctional Institute in Jackson.

It was an exhausting effort. People were getting soaked. No one was sleeping much. Even top officials were involved in overseeing the rescue. And that's how the secretary of corrections of Louisiana and the warden of Dixon Correctional Institute happened to be in a vehicle together, driving through the waterlogged streets of New Orleans headed for those buses. They were looking down the interstate, which was under water, when they spied two little eyes staring up at them.

Oh, no! They were physically tapped out. They had just gotten dry.

But the owner of those eyes was barely keeping his head above water. They just couldn't leave him to die. They fished the little Pomeranian out and had him transported to safety. He was named Evac. The deputy secretary of corrections of Louisiana adopted that dog.

Okay, you say, that's a great story—but it's a story of a dog *being* rescued, not *doing* the rescuing. Ahhh, but the story doesn't end there. Those two corrections officials started thinking and talking. They knew many other pets were homeless and in danger in Katrina's aftermath. A main shelter was being set up but couldn't handle the full workload. Dixon Correctional Institute volunteered to assist. Dixon had an agricultural program that included land and barns. They had prisoner manpower. Why not house some of these displaced pets there until they could either be reclaimed by their owners or placed in new homes?

That is exactly what they did. Countless animals were saved. Little did anyone know at that time how significant a role pet rescue would play in the future. This initial program morphed into others. With the help of prison labor and a Humane Society grant, Dixon built a no-kill animal shelter and an emergency evacuation facility and clinic right on its grounds. The shelter helps not only needy animals, it has helped rescue inmates whose hearts are softened as they work with these four-footed orphans. Pen Pals Inc. Animal Shelter is nonprofit, and it even has its own Facebook page.

I believe God's hand was in this. He has always been in the business of redeeming and transforming those some might discount as throwaways. He used a small, soggy hurricane victim to turn on a lightbulb in just the right people, birthing a program that has meant second chances for both animals and humans.

God also used a crippled woman on a street in Morocco to spotlight a need to a passing American tourist. But for that tourist, my dear friend Don, the lightbulb that would transform half a million lives and counting wouldn't fully turn on until 20 years later.

Don and his wife, Laurie, went on that Morocco trip early in their marriage. One day they saw a crippled woman trying to cross a street. She was crawling on the ground, dragging herself between people's legs. No one was doing anything to help her. It was as if they were used to the sight and didn't feel there was any way they could help. Don didn't help either…not then. But the scene stuck with him.

Don and Laurie finished their trip. They went home. They started a family and had three daughters. They were sending them to private schools. They were working hard. They were spending money to live the proverbial American dream. That dream started to crowd their spiritual life. They weren't praying. They were too busy to go to church much anymore.

Then, 20 years after that Morocco trip, their American dream fell to pieces.

The crisis that cracked Don's heart open to God's leading was his oldest daughter's struggle with an eating disorder. It would go on for five years. It would reveal to Don and Laurie what was wrong with the way they were living. It would take them to the end of themselves, drive them to seek the Lord, and show them what it was like to feel loved by Him. This, and a bout of cancer for Laurie, would bring the family back to prayer and church. And that was where Don would hear the sermon that turned a spotlight on the memory of that crawling woman and what God wanted Don to do about it.

Don's pastor talked about how each of us has God-given abilities for a purpose. One way to find God's will for us is to think about what needs there are that our abilities might meet. By profession, Don was a mechanical engineer. His work involved medical applications of those skills. He also had a fascination with wheelchairs, including antique versions from the Civil War.

Don thought about his mechanical engineering skills. He thought about that Moroccan woman crawling across the road. And he started working to design a different kind of wheelchair.

Don's idea was to craft a wheelchair for the poorest of the poor. Its cost would be low. It would be "one size fits all." It would hold up in different kinds of weather. And although it would be far from perfect, it would lift people up off the ground and give them the gift of mobility.

Evac the dog sparked a shelter program. The Moroccan crawler sparked a nonprofit organization, Free Wheelchair Mission. They have been in existence over ten years now. They have refined the initial wheelchair and created a second-generation version that has some limited adjustability. They have given away over half a million wheelchairs to the poorest of the poor all over the world. Those half a million plus lives, and Don's and Laurie's, will never be the same.

Evac and the Moroccan crawler were instrumental in rescuing others even though they couldn't save themselves. The same was true of a certain Samaritan woman we read about in John 4. She was at her local well when she encountered a Jew who did the unthinkable. He spoke with her and asked her for a drink of water.

Back then, in the first century, Jews normally wouldn't have anything to do with Samaritans. But this Jew, Jesus, began to talk with her. To her amazement, He knew all about her. He knew her sin. He spotlighted her need. And when she wondered if He was a prophet, He revealed He was far more. He was Messiah. Then this woman went back to her town and told a tale that led the rest to the only One who could redeem them.

Whoever thought a half-drowned dog, a helpless cripple, and a sin-soaked Samaritan would be instruments of rescue to so many others? But then again, who has the mind of God? He works in unexpected ways. Who knows how He might use you to bless others if you have eyes and ears to recognize His call.

> *Then I heard the voice of the Lord saying, "Whom shall I send? And who will go for us?"*
> *And I said, "Here am I. Send me!" (Isaiah 6:8).*

CONSIDER THIS:

What special gifts and abilities has God given you? What needs has He laid on your heart? Have you prayed and asked Him how He might want to bring these together?

Part IV

Comfort Is a Warm Puppy

Honey

A Spoonful of Honey
God's Encouragement Lifts Us Up

Where there is great love, there are always miracles.
WILLA CATHER

Honey the cocker spaniel never met Mary Poppins the nanny. She never heard that sugar is supposed to help medicine go down. But in her own most delightful way, she has sweetened reading for both children and adults. And in the process, some magical things have happened.

One of those magical things was something of a Christmas miracle. Honey and her human mom, Elizabeth, had been visiting a classroom of special needs children so they could read to Honey. One little boy who was autistic was scared of Honey. He would not get near her at first. He would just flap his arms up and down and say "Dog." He never spoke a sentence—and never had.

Nine weeks went by. Then one day the child took a therapist's hand and pulled her over to Honey. He put his hand down as if to touch the dog, but jerked it back. The boy did this three times. Then he looked at Honey and said, "I love you, Honey." He repeated it two or three times while his therapist's jaw dropped. Later, when Elizabeth and Honey were leaving, this same child came to the door, stuck his head around it, and told Honey he loved her one more time.

Elizabeth wasn't sure if the child understood the dog's name was Honey. She was about to find out. The next week was the week before Christmas. The boy said nothing the whole time Elizabeth and Honey were in his class. But as they were preparing to leave, he grabbed Elizabeth's hand, bent as if to pet the dog, stood back up, and said, "Merry Christmas, Honey."

Nor was Christmas the end of this miracle. Elizabeth has a fun way to treat both Honey and those who read to her. She cuts up carrots and lets each person feed a couple of carrot pieces to the dog both before and after reading. The week after Christmas, this little boy threw carrots on the floor, which Honey gobbled up. As Elizabeth was leaving that day, the boy danced from one foot to the other and announced, "Honey eats carrots."

Honey was the first living being this child had ever spoken a sentence to. Doing so was a huge breakthrough. The boy's family moved away, and Elizabeth lost contact with them, but she will never forget the experience she had. She said, simply, "God put me there." It's a highlight of her life.

Honey and Elizabeth are part of the R.E.A.D. program. R.E.A.D. stands for "Reading Education Assistance Dogs." To participate, Honey had to be a certified therapy dog. Honey lends a listening ear to readers in both public and parochial schools and visits a local library as well. She also works with special needs children and adults. Each reading session is normally 15 minutes long.

Small steps are huge for kids in the special needs classroom. Elizabeth recalls how another child came over, lay down next to Honey, hugged her, and fell asleep beside her on the floor. Elizabeth learned that this child normally wouldn't touch people or let them touch her. A third child always had her fists clenched. But when a therapist took the girl's hand and rubbed Honey's back, the child relaxed enough that her hand came open.

Honey is also beloved by students in the adult special needs class she visits. Their teacher said they don't always want to read, but they look forward to reading to the dog. One adult can't read at all but wants to spend time with Honey, so Elizabeth reads to him.

Elizabeth's own life has been sweetened by her experience in the R.E.A.D. program. She has health challenges that forced her to retire, but her work with Honey has changed her perspective. She takes new joy in her own life and feels closer to God knowing she and Honey can help others.

As I thought about Honey's encouraging presence and what it accomplished, it reminded me of Barnabas in the New Testament book of Acts. His given name was actually Joseph, but Barnabas was what everyone called him. Acts says the meaning of this name is "son of encouragement."

Barnabas was clearly an encourager. When Paul first returned to Jerusalem after his conversion, Christians there were leery of him. He had persecuted the early church, and they weren't at all sure they could trust him. But Barnabas came to Paul's rescue and convinced the others that Paul's profession of faith was real.

Later, God called both Paul and Barnabas to the church at Antioch and to go out together on missionary journeys. Interestingly, they eventually had a falling-out that itself had to do with encouragement. A young man named John Mark had accompanied them on their first journey and had let them down. Paul didn't want to take him along again. Barnabas saw it differently. The pair split up, and Barnabas continued to mentor Mark. He must have worked some magic there, because Mark went on to write a book of the Bible and apparently changed Paul's impression of him. When Paul needed help toward the end of his life, he wrote to Timothy, "Get Mark and bring him with you, because he is helpful to me in my ministry" (2 Timothy 4:11).

Honey and Barnabas, in very different ways, demonstrate how encouragement rescues. It's a spoonful of sweetness that makes life easier to bear. It can sometimes unlock and free us in unexpected and seemingly miraculous ways. A magical nanny named Mary Poppins isn't the only one who knows this. God surely does—He wired us this way. He delights to encourage us and to use us to encourage each other. Will you be someone's spoonful of honey today?

You, Lord, hear the desire of the afflicted;
you encourage them, and you listen to their cry.
(Psalm 10:17)

CONSIDER THIS:

How has God or another person given you a spoonful of
honey that helped you through a tough situation? What hap-
pened? How were you encouraged? How did it make a differ-
ence? How can you encourage others in God's name?

Wonderful Doggie Counselor
"Being There" Rescues

To be kind is sometimes more important than to be
right. Many times, what people need is not a brilliant
mind that speaks but a special heart that listens.

AUTHOR UNKNOWN

Hendrix the dog didn't have a degree in psychology, of course, but that didn't stop him from being a wonderful counselor to a host of hurting humans. What was his secret? He listened with his heart. He sensed when someone was in distress, and he cared. That's how he came to do therapy on his human mom SJ's grad-school friend who was terrified of dogs.

This friend of SJ's was so frightened she would shake when a canine came near. Hendrix sensed this and started working with her. Each time the friend visited, Hendrix crept just a little closer. Finally, one day, he got his head right up next to the dog-phobic object of his affections. With some trepidation, she reached over and hesitantly petted him. Finding that Hendrix enjoyed the attention and nothing awful happened to her, she was encouraged to repeat the gesture. Over time, her hesitation faded. The petting continued.

Hendrix sensed when people were upset, and he had ways of reaching out. One was to go and sit at a person's feet. SJ would discover that the individual had had a bad day. People would seek the dog out for this comfort. They would call SJ and ask, "Can I come over? I need to see Hendrix."

At other times, Hendrix would try to initiate contact with the hurting person. He would go over, turn around, and put himself in petting position. If the individual didn't respond, he would give the person a steady stare, as if to say, "I am here for you."

SJ is now a professor at a university in Texas. At an earlier point in her life, she was college master for the honors residential college at this school. There were 353 men and women, and SJ lived on site. Hendrix loved and was loved—and ministered to students in need. They would come to SJ and say, "Can I take Hendrix for a walk? I'm having a hard time." To thank the dog, they had a "Celebrate Hendrix Day" complete with a trail of doggie bones and biscuits.

Hendrix reached out to any and all in need, but he was always there for his beloved SJ. He stuck close through all of life's rough times and bumps. He was there when relationships crumbled. He sat by her side as she was writing her dissertation—and brought his leash when the printer turned off.

Hendrix lived an amazing 17 plus years, and when his time came, SJ sensed he was trying to hang on for her and needed to be released. On a Thursday, she told Hendrix she would be okay. As much as she didn't want him to go, she'd be upset if he stayed and wound up hurting himself. She told him he didn't have to get up anymore if he didn't want to. The next morning, for the first time ever, Hendrix stayed in his bed. He stopped eating. The following Monday, SJ took him to the vet, spent some precious last love time with him, and had him put to sleep.

We humans don't always do as faithful and consistent a job as Hendrix, even though we might want to. I am reminded of Jesus's disciples in the Garden of Gethsemane. While Jesus agonized in prayer, they fell into an exhausted sleep. Later, when He was arrested, they fled.

Jesus understood their weakness—and ours. He has given His Holy Spirit to His children. He has empowered us to "be there" for a hurting world. In 2 Corinthians 1:3-5 (MSG) Paul says:

All praise to the God and Father of our Master, Jesus the Messiah! Father of all mercy! God of all healing counsel! He comes alongside us when we go through hard times, and before you know it, he brings us alongside someone else who is going through hard times so that we can be there for that person just as God was there for us. We have plenty of hard times that come from following the Messiah, but no more so than the good times of his healing comfort—we get a full measure of that, too.

Hendrix the dog got an awful lot done for a canine with a limited life span who couldn't be in more than one place at a time. His loving presence rescued countless humans around him. Nor did he choose the objects of his love by their response to him. He chose them by the need he sensed in their hearts.

How much more might we be used as God's children if we allow His love to fill us and His Spirit to lead us? We don't need to have all the answers either. Often we can do far more by just being there to listen and care—as Hendrix was.

May your unfailing love be my comfort,
according to your promise to your servant.
(Psalm 119:76)

CONSIDER THIS:

Have you ever been in crisis and felt rescued by the loving presence of another? How was this person there for you? How did God show His presence and love through them or directly? How might you use this to comfort someone else?

A Doggie Bridge of Comfort
God Bridges Our Chasms

Love builds bridges where there are none.
R.H. DELANEY

La vie is French for life—and La Vie the golden retriever has given new life to others. He has been a living bridge of comfort for those who are hurting. He has lent a helping paw in hospital rooms and in the court system. And he has also helped his beloved master, Scott, move past a lost dream to a ministry filled with meaning and purpose.

The loss of that dream had its roots in Scott's childhood. He had polio as a youngster. All four of his limbs were paralyzed. He recovered, but around age 40, he began to have problems doctors attributed to post-polio syndrome. Among other things, the use of his left hand became limited. He had to give up his dream of becoming a professional golfer. Over time, his day job became less satisfying as well. But he'd given his heart to Jesus at age 36, and he had always loved animals, especially dogs. In 2002 he had two special prayer requests for the Lord. He wanted to retire from his long-term career, and he dreamed of getting a golden retriever and doing pet therapy work.

In 2003, God answered Scott's first prayer with an amazing buy-out offer from his employer. In 2004, God gave him La Vie.

Scott remembers laying hands on La Vie, whose call name is L.A., the very first night he got the pup. He prayed, *Lord, he is Your gift, and I ask that You use him in a mighty way*. Even Scott did not dream how amazing a pet therapy journey God would take them on together.

Scott and L.A. began that journey at a local hospital, St. Joseph's, when the pup was just 19 weeks old. Technically, L.A. was too young to be let in, but the hospital had lost the guidelines that governed this. When Scott called and told them his pup did things even he could not explain, they said to bring him on down. L.A. got approved to visit patients, even though he was still so small they had to put him on a chair to take his picture for his badge.

From the first day he set foot, or should I say paw, in the hospital, this dog has been wonderful. He would go up to a two- or three-year-old child, sniff the youngster, then lie down and roll over for a belly rub. Scott never trained him to do this—it was all L.A.'s idea. Scott became the facility's first, and so far only, Pet Therapy Chairman. Over the past eight years, Scott and L.A. have touched many lives, but a couple of stories stand out.

The first involved a child in the Pediatric Intensive Care Unit (PICU). It began three days before Christmas. Scott and L.A. had been visiting patients elsewhere in the hospital, and they were bushed. But they usually stopped by the PICU mostly for the mutual benefit of the hospital staff and the dog. Patients were usually too ill for L.A. to visit, but seeing him helped the staff relax, and two of the nurses would get on the floor and give the tired canine a massage. A charge nurse even kept dog treats for him.

As they were leaving the PICU to go home, they passed a woman in the hall on her cell phone. It turned out her child was a patient there. She asked if they'd gone into the room where her husband and daughter were. No, they hadn't—the room was dark. Mom pleaded with them to visit. Her little girl would love it!

Tired as they were, Scott complied. The girl, who we'll call Janie, was lying on her side. It was a high bed. To Scott's surprise, L.A. jumped up onto the end of it, something he didn't normally do.

The dad explained that Janie was partially paralyzed. Scott told L.A.

to crawl. The little girl started trying to pet the dog. Dad was crying. He said it was the first time she had moved in two days. No one else had been able to get her to budge.

Scott and L.A. hung out in the room for a short time and then asked if the family would like them to return the next day. They were delighted.

Janie was sitting up in bed, waiting, when Scott and L.A. showed up. Family members were with her. L.A. did tricks in the bed and she loved it. Janie was trying to move and using her good side quite a bit. She was happy but starting to wear out, and Scott knew it was time to go. Her family was in tears. Mom told Scott that the visit with the dog was the greatest Christmas gift they could have gotten.

The second story is about a little girl with leukemia. Desi and her mom loved Jesus. They'd first met Scott and L.A. when the child was hospitalized. Later, when Desi had to return for chemotherapy, her mom asked for L.A. to come and visit her. L.A. couldn't be present during the treatments, but he could spend time with Desi beforehand. They did this in a small meeting room near the treatment rooms, where L.A. loved on the girl. Her mom told Scott the visits helped her daughter get through. Every time she saw the dog before a treatment, she had a good day. As of this writing, Desi is in remission.

L.A. is a registered therapy dog, and he and Scott work through a national pet therapy organization. They have gone through training and testing and there are regulations governing what they do. There are also guidelines for bathing the dog before he makes hospital visits, since germs and sanitation are huge concerns. But it has been a joy for Scott and L.A. to work in the hospital setting, and they have brought untold comfort and joy to others.

More recently, Scott's and L.A.'s ministry has extended to the local court system. The state attorney wanted a dog program there, and L.A.'s role is to be a reassuring and relaxing presence for children. Usually it is an intake situation. There has been an incident, and a child will come in with a caregiver or the parents. A social worker or lawyer will question the child, and during the questioning, the parent or caregiver can't be present, but the dog can.

The normal format is that Scott and L.A. are introduced to the youngster, and Scott will explain to the accompanying grown-up what they do. He lets the youngster get used to L.A. and asks things like, "Do you have a dog? Would you like to pet L.A.? He does tricks; would you like to see one?"

During the questioning of the child, L.A. usually just lies down, but kids can choose to interact with him. Scott says the dog's presence changes the whole atmosphere. And every once in a while L.A. will get up and nudge a child's arm. Typically it's when the youngster is having it rough.

Scott still remembers the very first time he and L.A. sat in on a case. It involved a 13-year-old girl who had been abused. She hardly seemed to be L.A.'s biggest fan, but Scott learned otherwise after the girl took a walk with her mom on a break. The mom later told Scott that her daughter could not stop talking about L.A. and the work Scott and his dog were doing.

If a dog whose heart is as golden as his coat could bring such comfort, how much more can our "God of all comfort" do? When it comes to bridging our chasms of hurt and pain and helplessness, Paul's words to the Corinthians are telling. In 2 Corinthians 4:8-10, he writes, "We are hard pressed on every side, but not crushed; perplexed, but not in despair; persecuted, but not abandoned; struck down, but not destroyed. We always carry around in our body the death of Jesus, so that the life of Jesus may also be revealed in our body."

L.A. has done his doggie best for kids needing comfort, and he made a big difference in their lives. But he isn't God. Jesus is! He cared so much about our rough times that He gave His life to save us. He bridged the chasm of sin and death and is our forever Living Bridge over any troubled waters this life or the devil can send us. Will you be like Paul and stand on Him?

When hard pressed, I cried to the Lord;
  he brought me into a spacious place.
The Lord *is with me; I will not be afraid.*
  What can mere mortals do to me?
                              (Psalm 118:5-6)

CONSIDER THIS:

What is the deepest chasm or most troubled water you have ever faced? Did you have a living bridge of comfort to help you across? If so, who was it and how did they help? How has God been a living bridge of comfort in your life?

A Healing Paw in Loss
God's Touch Helps Us Through

When you cannot stand, He will bear you in His arms.
Francis de Sales

Laurie didn't know what she needed in the midst of her devastating loss. She just knew her heart was flooded with grief. Her first child, a boy, had lived only eight hours. His umbilical cord had been knotted, and his body wastes had leaked into the amniotic fluid. When the infant started to breathe, he aspirated this. The resulting pneumonia claimed his life.

Because she'd had an emergency C-section, Laurie had to stay home for five weeks. Her husband, Don, had to get back to work, however. She was alone with an empty baby room and her tears.

But before her world fell apart, Laurie and Don had reserved a newborn husky puppy. They didn't have a dog yet, and she'd thought it was a great time to get one. It was winter, they lived in Boston, and she'd be home with the baby anyway.

Two weeks into her grieving process, it was time for Laurie to pick up the puppy they named Mika. After a day with her new dog, Laurie realized this was the first day she hadn't wept. Looking back, she realizes the pup was God's provision. They got close right away. Holding

Mika, caring for her, loving and being loved by her sweet dog helped get Laurie through. Mika was with them for 12 years and helped them welcome three more now-grown children into the world.

My new friend Cindy would not be at all surprised by Laurie's story. She and her therapy dogs have teamed as grief facilitators. First Andy and then Cathal, both Staffordshire bull terriers, have helped to comfort grieving kids and adults and unlock their emotions so they could talk about their loss and move forward in a healthy way.

Andy was the very first therapy dog at a Wisconsin facility named MargaretAnn's Place. It was founded in memory of a 20-month-old who died suddenly. Its purpose is to provide a place for children to grieve. Cindy and Andy went to group sessions there twice a month for over ten years.

Cindy remembers how Andy reached out to a grandfather who brought his granddaughter in. They were grieving the loss of the little girl's brother. Granddad was struggling with his emotions and had no intentions of staying. Andy was with a large group of kids who were petting him. He got up and went to the man, who remarked that the only ones who liked him were kids and dogs. Andy returned to the children, but he soon went back to the granddad and put his paws up on the fellow. The man's resistance melted under the dog's love. He began to hug and pet Andy. He decided to stay after all and went into a group for adults.

Then there was the teenage boy who'd lost his mom at age three. He'd been in and out of grief groups for about five years. Andy crawled up in his lap and kissed him. Tears fell from the boy's eyes. He'd hit some speed bumps, but perhaps thanks in part to a helping paw from Andy, he began to get back on track.

Andy helped another teen deal with tragically unfinished business. Her dad had died in a work accident. They'd had an argument the night before, and now she couldn't tell him she was sorry. Andy curled up in this girl's lap. She hugged him and held him and was able to open up about her feelings. She kept coming to the group and now, years later, is all grown up with a family of her own.

Just the mere presence of a dog creates a homier, more welcoming atmosphere in a grief group, Cindy told me. Andy was also a constant in these kids' lives. They knew when they went to the group, he would be there waiting for them. Being able to count on that was very comforting at a time when the rest of their world had been turned upside down by loss.

There were also special activities to help the kids deal with their feelings. One involved putting red and pink hearts in a vest. Andy always wore a special vest when he was working, and it had a zippered pocket. Cindy invited the kids to write the name of the person they'd lost on one side of a paper heart. On the other side, they could put their own name. They would then tuck the hearts in Andy's pocket so he could keep them safe.

For the last two years of Andy's life, he also went with Cindy to a grief camp called Camp Erin®. Part of the experience is a special Saturday night candlelight ceremony. Each child decorates a star, puts a candle in the middle, and launches their star onto a lake. Andy's last time there, he stood on shore and cried. Afterward, one little boy was especially moved and sat on the dock with his cabin counselor long after the other kids had gone. Andy went and sat beside him and wouldn't leave till he did.

Some things about grief work can be taught. Others are innate. Andy had a heart to be there and care. He could sense who needed him and eagerly gave himself to those who were grieving and hurting.

After many years with her wonderful dog, Cindy is now grieving Andy's recent passing from nasal cancer. Many others miss him too. Cindy got a flood of sympathy cards—even more than when she lost her father two years earlier.

Andy has passed his baton to Cathal. Cindy made this real to the kids in a marvelous way. She took the hearts from Andy's vest and zipped them into Cathal's vest pocket. It's now his turn to keep those hearts safe and extend a healing paw to those who are grieving.

Andy's empathy brings to mind what Paul urged the Romans to do for those in grief. Paul told them to "mourn with those who mourn" (Romans 12:15). That is exactly what Jesus did when His dear friend

Lazarus died—even though He knew Lazarus wouldn't stay dead very long.

Jesus loved Lazarus and his sisters, Mary and Martha. When their brother took sick, the women sent for Jesus. But He waited two days to go to them. Why? Jesus told His disciples, "This sickness will not end in death. No, it is for God's glory so that God's Son may be glorified through it" (John 11:4).

By the time Jesus arrived in Bethany, Lazarus had already been in a tomb for four days. First Martha went to greet the Lord. Then she sent Mary to speak with Him. Though the sisters had some level of faith in Jesus, neither quite realized what He was about to do.

What happened next is a beautiful picture of God's compassion and love. Mary wept and some Jewish mourners with her wept also. Then Jesus wept too. Scripture doesn't actually tell us why. But I believe He cared about and shared the grief of those He loved, even though He knew He was about to raise Lazarus from the dead as a foretaste of His own resurrection.

Jesus put arms and legs on God's love—not just then but throughout His life. And now that He has gone to the Father, we are to do that for each other. But in addition, He has given us wonderful four-pawed friends to help us deal with our earthly loss.

He has given us much more, however. He has given us a picture of our future hope. Lazarus rose, but he died again. Jesus rose and ascended to the Father. And one day all those who have trusted in Him will join Him in the Father's presence forever.

Meanwhile we grieve for those who have left us because separation hurts. And we can take our pain to a caring God. Whether it's through the love of a dog, the tears and embrace of a caring friend, or the gentle ministry of His Spirit and His Word, He is waiting to comfort us and hold us close to Him.

Even though I walk
  through the darkest valley,
I will fear no evil,
  for you are with me;
your rod and your staff,
  they comfort me.
            (Psalm 23:4)

CONSIDER THIS:

When is the last time you lost a beloved person or pet? What was hardest to deal with? Who helped you through? What brought you comfort? Is there someone who might need your loving presence in loss?

How Dogs Set Prisoners Free
God Unlocks Our Chains

We are all serving a life sentence
in the dungeon of the self.
CYRIL CONNOLLY

Roxie the beagle was trapped in a prison. It wasn't the no-kill shelter in Maine where she was originally housed, Pope Memorial Humane Society of Knox County. It wasn't the men's prison where she was sent for training, either. What held her captive was her own fear. And by letting a human prisoner break through her shell and start freeing her, she helped to free him too.

Roxie had been found abandoned and chained to a fence. She was so scared, she would shake when people came near her. The shelter staff didn't know if she'd been mistreated or just hadn't had good puppy socialization. What they did know was that she stood a much better chance of being adopted if she became less timid and nervous. They put her into their K-9 Corrections program.

K-9 Corrections teams shelter dogs with nonviolent offenders at a minimum-security men's correctional facility. Participants are chosen through an application process. Dogs in the program have both a primary and a secondary handler. Each selected dog goes to live with its inmate handlers in their room, and they care for and work with the pup under professional guidance.

Roxie was assigned to a primary handler named John, who was serving a drug-related sentence. John's missteps had cost him and others dearly, and he felt deep remorse. He was looking to rebuild his life, and he soon realized his new four-pawed friend was helping him do just that.

Marie, who works with both men and dogs in the program, told me John doted on Roxie. It made him feel good to watch Roxie blossom. She bonded with him and her secondary handler, was extremely affectionate, and did well in training. Back at the shelter, she got adopted into a home with three other beagles. "She was still nervous and timid at times, but she had more coping skills," Marie explained. Since her adoption, Roxie was even boarded at a vet clinic and did well.

Another dog who got under John's skin was a big black Labrador named Walker. At first, the pooch had a mind of his own. John worked with him for five months. It was hard to break through, but John did. Walker calmed down and learned his commands. He got a home with a couple from out of state, and they wrote and thanked John for his work with the dog. They said Walker was a great addition to their family. They even tucked some photos into the envelope. John wound up corresponding with them, and they still have a relationship.

John helped open up a wonderful new world for Roxie and Walker and other dogs he worked with. They returned the favor. They helped him realize he wanted to do more with animals. He asked to do community service at the shelter. It took some months, but in the end he got approved. Once at the shelter, John continued to learn new things and also began to develop lasting relationships in his life.

At this writing, John is finishing his sentence through a special program that allows him to live and work in the community under supervision. He must have a sponsor and check in with a probation officer. He is working at the shelter for pay, and an employee of the shelter and her husband are sponsoring and housing John, and he is very grateful.

John isn't sure what his future holds, but he told me he likes the life he built and might want to do this kind of thing long-term. Working at the shelter has also eased his reentry into normal life. People from the community who meet him at the shelter greet him when they see him on the street.

John's four-pawed pals from K-9 Corrections helped give him hope and a future. The same was also true for an inmate named Thomas.

Thomas was serving a sentence for drug-related charges too. He'd gotten cancer at age 21, and he became addicted to his pain meds and kept taking them even after the cancer was gone. When he bounced checks to pay for them, he got busted.

Thomas applied for K-9 Corrections hoping it would make his prison time pass faster. It did that and much more. A very special pit-bull puppy named Daisy helped Thomas reconnect in a deeper way with his own little boy.

Daisy was just ten weeks old when Thomas started to work with her. She was untrained and rambunctious. She was also into "resource guarding"—she would store toys in her kennel.

Thomas had to potty-train Daisy. When he'd first been sent to prison, his then toddler son was potty-training age. Working with Daisy took him back to that period. Dog training also gave him something to talk about that grabbed his now four-year-old's attention. Their nightly phone visits, which had lasted just a couple of minutes, started extending to a quarter of an hour. The little boy was all ears to learn how Daisy was doing. The pup did well enough in her three months with Thomas that she got adopted into a nice home afterward.

Thomas told me he'd suffered from anxiety his whole life. His work with Daisy and other shelter dogs helped that. It also helped him see people in a whole different light. He watched fellow prisoners get on their knees and talk to a dog as if it were a baby. It made him more comfortable with them and taught him not to judge a book by its cover.

Thomas was also given a chance to work at the animal shelter. His four-pawed charges helped him find a missing piece of himself. He'd always loved helping others, but the drug addiction had stolen that and turned his focus inward. No more. Now on home release, Thomas wants to take a 38-week college course to become a substance abuse counselor. He is also volunteering with the Special Olympics. And though he now lives some distance away, he still volunteers at the shelter when he can.

John and Thomas may have served time in a physical prison, but their deeper prison was an inner one. And they're not the only ones. In Galatians 3:22 (NLT) the apostle Paul wrote, "But the Scriptures declare that we are all prisoners of sin, so we receive God's promise of freedom only by believing in Jesus Christ."

Because Paul understood this truth, he was able to free others even while a physical prisoner himself. That's what he did when he was jailed in Philippi. Paul had cast a demon out of a slave girl who was a fortune-teller. Her fortune-telling had been a cash cow for her masters, and they weren't happy when she lost that ability. They hurled accusations at Paul and his companion, Silas, and both were flogged and thrown into jail.

Regardless of their physical plight, Paul and Silas were free in their hearts. Their focus was outward, not inward. They were praying and singing hymns at midnight while other prisoners listened. Then a violent earthquake hit. Prisoners' chains were shaken loose and the jail doors flew open. Acts 16:27-30 tells us what happened next:

> The jailer woke up, and when he saw the prison doors open, he drew his sword and was about to kill himself because he thought the prisoners had escaped. But Paul shouted, "Don't harm yourself! We are all here!"
>
> The jailer called for lights, rushed in and fell trembling before Paul and Silas. He then brought them out and asked, "Sirs, what must I do to be saved?"

Paul led the jailer and his whole household to the Lord and eternal freedom, and they were baptized that very night.

Roxie, Walker, and Daisy brought freedom to prisoners in an earthly sense. They helped their handlers reconnect with others and experience the joy of giving. Just by being their doggie selves, they helped to break the inner chains of the men who worked with them and grew to love them. But it took God to break spiritual chains of sin and death—and He was willing. He sent His Son into this world to live a sinless life and die as an innocent sacrifice to free us all. Through faith in Him, we receive the ultimate correction—a new nature—and are welcomed into God's eternal family forever.

Have you received the freedom He offers?

> *God sets the lonely in families,*
>   *he leads out the prisoners with singing;*
>   *but the rebellious live in a sun-scorched land.*
>   *(Psalm 68:6)*

CONSIDER THIS:

Who or what has held you prisoner in your life? Who or what has freed you? How has God freed you? How might you help free others?

Ihana's Chicken Soup
Compassion Rescues

Frequently people think compassion and love are merely
sentimental. No! They are very demanding. If you are
going to be compassionate, be prepared for action!
Desmond Tutu

Wendy didn't get a dog to be rescued from a midlife crisis. She did it more for safety reasons. She loved walking in the woods near her rural Maryland home. When she borrowed her neighbor's Labrador for such jaunts, she felt more secure. That made her long to be walked by a dog of her own.

After researching different breeds, Wendy was drawn to Weimaraners. They were billed as great companion dogs. She decided to rescue one and put in an adoption application with the Washington, DC, Weimaraner club.

When the club got back to her, they had three dogs to choose from. Two were males from the same owner, needing re-homing. The third was a female with an unknown past. The club suspected she had escaped from a puppy mill. She had been pregnant and had given birth to a litter. There were indications she had been severely abused. She would definitely be a time-intensive dog.

Christmas was coming and Wendy had plans to be out of town, so she waited till after the holidays to make a choice. She asked to meet the female. When she did, she knew. This severely underweight, mistreated pooch was *hers*! She took her new dog home and named her Ihana—the Finnish word for "beautiful."

Wendy thought she was rescuing Ihana. What she soon realized was that Ihana was also rescuing her. She had been struggling with a sort of midlife depression. Her biological clock was ticking and she longed to be married, but it just wasn't happening. Had God forgotten her? Did He really care about her?

Ihana became a visible, tangible touch from God in Wendy's life. She made Wendy live in the present. She was a living, breathing being that Wendy could talk to. She forced Wendy into a regular routine. The unconditional love of this dog made God's unconditional love more real. Not only did Wendy choose Ihana, but Ihana chose Wendy too. Ihana was Wendy's emotional "chicken soup." Her faithful love helped rescue Wendy from her doldrums and restore her confidence in God's faithfulness and care.

Over time, Wendy also discovered that Ihana could be a healing presence in other people's lives. For the past few years, she has been a therapy dog. Wendy put her through training with Pets on Wheels. Ihana had to learn to ignore distractions and take treats with a soft mouth. She had to learn what to do around walkers and wheelchairs. She had to know her basic commands (sit, down, stay). But there were things Pets on Wheels could not teach—elements of compassion that Ihana displayed in ways that surprised even her adoring master.

Wendy takes Ihana to visit the residents of a nursing home. Many of them once had pets and miss them greatly. It cheers their hearts to see Ihana, and Wendy says her dog seems to have an uncanny way of sensing what each one needs. Though Ihana doesn't normally give Wendy kisses, she gives kisses to some of these residents—and she seems to know just who will like it. One gentleman would get out of his wheelchair to greet the dog. He once rushed out to meet Ihana with shaving cream all over his face.

Making this kind of emotional connection is draining for Ihana. Wendy says her dog can do this for only about an hour at a time.

Ihana's gift of compassion extends to animals as well. She never seemed to want a canine companion, but then she got a bad infection, and Wendy feared she might lose Ihana. Maybe it was time to look into rescuing a second pooch.

The result of Wendy's new search was a five-year-old male Weimaraner named Cooper. He hadn't had the easiest early life. She discovered he'd been terrorized by small dogs and was aggressive toward other dogs, including Ihana. Wendy has had to discipline him and work with him, but he is much better, and she feels Ihana is part of the reason. "Ihana has done wonders in helping him, no question. She gives him his space and is no longer afraid of him. They are often seen on the same couch together and seem to care for each other."

Wendy recalls a time a few months ago when she was eating outside with a friend and Cooper was "fence fighting" with the neighbor's dog. Finally, she got tired of disciplining him and put him in the garage. "Ihana was so shocked! She lay down on the other side of the door and waited for him to be let out of his prison. I think they were nose to nose through the door. She's definitely alpha now between them, and he lets her correct him when he doesn't listen."

Scripture tells us that our God is loving, compassionate, and merciful. He may use people and even pets to show His compassion to those who are hurting and touch them with His healing presence. There are countless biblical examples, including the prayer of compassion from the Hebrew prophet Elijah to save a widow's son.

Israel was ruled by the evil King Ahab and had fallen into idolatry. God commanded Elijah to pronounce judgment (1 Kings 17). Elijah declared there would be a drought, and then God sent him into hiding. First, he went to a wilderness area where God used ravens to feed him. Then God told him to stay with a widow in Sidon. God provided food for them and all was going quite well until the widow's son became ill and finally stopped breathing.

The poor widow was beside herself. She asked Elijah, "What do you have against me, man of God? Did you come to remind me of my sin and kill my son?" (1 Kings 17:18).

Elijah was deeply distressed. He knew the pain this woman was in. He took the boy up to the room where he was staying, stretched his own body over the child three times, and begged God for his life.

God had compassion on the child. The boy came back from the dead, and Elijah returned him to his mother. God's compassion working through Elijah not only healed the son's body, it healed that mother's heart. It was emotional chicken soup. She told the prophet, "Now I know that you are a man of God and that the word of the LORD from your mouth is the truth" (1 Kings 17:24).

God used Ihana to show Wendy He cares and to rescue her heart. He used Elijah to show a widow the same. He longs to pour out His compassion through each of us as well. You might be just the chicken soup some hurting heart needs, so listen for His leading and let Him love others through you.

Therefore, as God's chosen people, holy and dearly loved, clothe yourselves with compassion, kindness, humility, gentleness and patience (Colossians 3:12).

CONSIDER THIS:

Is there a time when compassion shown by a caring person or pet had a healing influence in your life? What happened? How did it help? How did it influence your relationship with God? How might you be God's chicken soup for someone else in need?

The Dog Who Chased Fear
God Is Our Refuge

There are more things to alarm us than to harm us,
and we suffer more often in apprehension than reality.
SENECA

On a never-to-be-forgotten April day in 1999, the concept of a shot heard 'round the world gained a new and awful meaning at a high school in Columbine, Colorado. Two troubled seniors shot up the campus, killing or wounding a number of students and then taking their own lives. The emotional aftershocks rippled far beyond those directly involved—and left one deeply affected California boy in need of rescue by a very special dog.

This dog, a three-year-old Dalmatian, had only recently been rescued himself. The boy's father, Randy, had spotted him crumpled by the side of the road in East Los Angeles. Randy pulled over, put on his hazard lights, and tried to approach. But the dog pulled himself up and fled.

Randy continued on to work, but the hurt dog weighed on his heart. After praying, he decided to go back and give his Good Samaritan mission one more try. He found the wounded Dalmatian under a bush. The big guy put his jaws around Randy's arm, but didn't bite.

Randy got the dog into his vehicle and took him to a vet. He was so muscular, the vet suspected he might have been bred for fighting. Perhaps he'd escaped that situation. Judging by the dog's physical condition, he might have been abused—or he might have been hit by a car. Either way, he had some healing to do.

That healing happened in Randy's care. He took the dog home to his wife and son and named him Rocky. As their new dog got better, they discovered he had some aggression issues. He respected Randy as his alpha or pack leader, but most other people were a different story. Randy's wife, Terri, had been bitten by a dog as a child and had some residual fears. In the beginning, she would run from room to room and close the door behind her to keep Rocky away. Still, though Rocky growled at her at times, he never, ever hurt her. Eventually, she grew comfortable with him. She believes God used them to help each other. But Rocky's most dramatic rescue work involved their son, Conner.

Conner had been a miracle child. Terri had suffered several miscarriages before conceiving him. He was born prematurely at just 26 weeks of age and weighed only one pound nine ounces. Against all odds, he survived. But he had some learning disabilities.

Though he had some challenges when processing information, Conner was just a normal kid in other ways. He loved people and music and animals. He especially loved Dalmatians—courtesy of a certain famous Disney movie about 101 of them. As a young child he had a stuffed Dalmatian he was so attached to, his mom had to sneak it away to wash it. He begged for a real-life version as a pet. But these were pricey dogs and didn't quite fit the budget. His mom told him to pray.

Five years later, enter Rocky! He and Conner became like brothers, tussling and playing together. Terri told Conner that God had answered. She believed the dog was from Him, in His perfect timing. Even she didn't guess how true that would prove to be in the days ahead.

About three months after Rocky joined the family, the Columbine shooting commandeered the news. Conner was not quite 11 years old. He was horrified by the tragedy and became extremely anxious and fearful. He was scared to go to school. He didn't want to be left alone even for a short time while his mom ran to the store. He didn't even want to take out the trash by himself, something he'd had no problem doing before.

Terri and Randy tried to calm Conner's fears. They even took him to a Christian counselor. Nothing seemed to make things better. Then they thought about Rocky. He was big and muscular and protective. Maybe they could use the dog to reassure their son.

Terri and Randy told Conner that his dog would keep him safe. They had him take Rocky when he went to dump the garbage. Mom or Dad would follow behind at a distance just to be sure neither boy nor dog ran into any problems, but they didn't let Conner see them. Terri also told Conner he'd be fine when she went to the store because Rocky was home with him. When she returned, he'd say, "Rocky protected me, Mom." Gradually, Conner's anxiety lessened until he reached the place where he was able to handle these things on his own again.

Rocky rescued Conner by his presence. Conner took emotional refuge in his dog. Metaphorically, Rocky was a fortress for this boy. As long as his dog was by his side, Conner felt protected and safe.

God is a fortress and refuge for His children too—and He wants us to believe that and trust in Him so we can feel comforted and protected also.

I love how so many psalms remind us that God's presence protects us. Psalm 46:1 tells us,

> God is our refuge and strength,
> an ever-present help in trouble.

Psalm 31:2-3 begs God,

> Turn your ear to me,
> come quickly to my rescue;
> be my rock of refuge,
> a strong fortress to save me.
> Since you are my rock and my fortress,
> for the sake of your name lead and guide me.

Though God is always with His children, usually He isn't visible to our naked eye. But there have been times when God has given His people a visual manifestation of His presence. He did this when the Israelites were in the wilderness.

> By day the LORD went ahead of them in a pillar of cloud to guide them on their way and by night in a pillar of fire to give them light, so that they could travel by day or night. Neither the pillar of cloud by day nor the pillar of fire by night left its place in front of the people (Exodus 13:21-22).

When the Egyptians chased after God's people to drag them back into slavery, He acted from that pillar to save them in dramatic fashion:

> The Egyptians pursued them, and all Pharaoh's horses and chariots and horsemen followed them into the sea. During the last watch of the night the LORD looked down from the pillar of fire and cloud at the Egyptian army and threw it into confusion. He jammed the wheels of their chariots so that they had difficulty driving. And the Egyptians said, "Let's get away from the Israelites! The LORD is fighting for them against Egypt" (Exodus 14:23-25).

Despite this and many other things God did to demonstrate His presence and protection, when it came time to go in and conquer Canaan, His people flunked their entrance exam. They didn't step out with God, as Conner did with Rocky. Because they feared giants instead of God, they were forced to wander in the wilderness until a new generation grew up that would enter the land by faith in Him.

It was a very different story when a priest named Ezra led a group of exiled Hebrews back to Jerusalem following the Babylonian captivity. He had the blessing of the Persian king, but he was leading a large group of people and they were bringing gold and silver for the temple as well. There was very real and present danger. But Ezra wrote,

> I was ashamed to ask the king for soldiers and horsemen to protect us from enemies on the road, because we had told

the king, "The gracious hand of our God is on everyone who looks to him, but his great anger is against all who forsake him." So we fasted and petitioned our God about this, and he answered our prayer (Ezra 8:22-23).

God protected Ezra's group from enemies and bandits, and they arrived safely at their destination with the treasure intact. Now, I'm not saying today's believers shouldn't take wise protective measures. But in this instance, God called Ezra to demonstrate His power and faithfulness to a pagan king, and Ezra trusted and obeyed.

God gave Conner a dog to help rescue him from his fears. But dogs don't live forever. Not long ago, Rocky passed from this world at the ripe old age of 16. Much as Conner grieved his loss, he knows his real protection is in the Lord, who will be at his side forever. Now grown up, he delights to praise God by playing drums in a church worship band.

God is bigger than what we fear—whether imaginary or real. He wants to rescue and comfort us with His presence. Will you hang back like those Israelites, or will you step out like Conner and Ezra and let Him be your fortress too?

> Trust in him at all times, you people;
>   pour out your hearts to him,
>   for God is our refuge.
>   *(Psalm 62:8)*

CONSIDER THIS:

Is there a fear you need rescuing from that's keeping you in the wilderness? Have you talked to God about it? How is it affecting you and your loved ones? Which of God's promises might help you step out, trusting He is by your side?

The Master of Disaster
Sometimes Wreckage Brings Rescue

There's no disaster that can't become a blessing,
and no blessing that can't become a disaster.
RICHARD BACH

If you had told Nicole's family a few years ago that they would be rescued by a 95-pound wrecking ball in a dog's body, they might not have believed you. Then they met Rudy, aka "the Master of Disaster."

Actually, the story begins with their previous pup, a beloved boxer named Barney. Nicole and her husband got Barney around the same time that she gave birth to their twin daughters. She didn't have baby monitors for them. Not to worry! Barney had those boxer nanny genes. He kept an eye and ear out for their needs. If Nicole was napping and the infants woke up hungry and started crying, he would run back and forth between their room and hers, barking, until she got up to nurse them.

As the twins grew a little older, Barney watched out for them in other ways. They lived in a two-story home, and the girls' bedroom was on the upper level. Though the door had a child safety lock, unbeknownst to Mom and Dad, their little ones had learned to pick it. One morning, Nicole woke up to strange sounds from Barney. When she went to check, she found both her toddlers out of their room, by the stairs, with Barney doing a body block. He was making scolding noises, placing himself between them and the steps, and nudging them away.

When the girls got old enough to swim in the pool, Barney appointed himself their four-legged lifeguard. He would run back and forth beside them, watching them for any sign of a problem. He would not leave them—not for food or anything else! He felt it was his job to protect them, and he did his doggie best.

This was one of the many reasons why his family was devastated when Barney got cancer at the age of eight. Due to the type of cancer, his vet didn't hold out much hope. They tried everything they could to save him, but a year later, Barney passed away.

Nicole and her family now had a huge dog-shaped hole in their lives. Even with two active children, their home felt much too quiet. They were all grieving and cried a lot. Nicole and her husband decided a new boxer pup was in order—one that came from healthy stock and had a great temperament. They began searching on the Internet and finally found some folks in Texas who were raising puppies they thought might suit their needs.

These folks were choosy about who got their litters. Nicole recalls that they had to write an essay about why they thought they would be good puppy parents. She described how they'd cooked for Barney and let him sleep on their bed. This seemed to please the Texas folks. But the three pups in their latest litter were already spoken for.

Barney had passed away in July. The new puppy application happened in early August. Nicole and her husband kept searching, but didn't find any other prospects. It got to be October. The Texas puppies were now old enough to go to their homes, but one puppy placement hit an unexpected glitch. The Texas breeders called Nicole's family. The male pup was theirs if they still wanted one and would pay his airfare.

Nicole and her husband didn't think twice. They happily paid for shipping and went to Los Angeles International Airport to collect their new pup, whose first act as a family member, after he relieved himself, was to chew on his new humans' sleeves!

That was five years ago. Nicole still cautions would-be visitors to their home that their now 95-pound pooch has a sleeve fetish. But that's far from the only thing Rudy will chomp. He has gnawed on Christmas tree lights and ornaments. He has "eaten" a couch. He once consumed four pounds of meat that was left unguarded for only a couple of minutes. He also gobbled an entire loaf of bread, leaving only a few crumbs and the bag. No matter! He has chewed—and loved and snuggled—his way into his adoring family's hearts to stay.

Oh, and that dog-shaped hole in the family? It has been filled to the brim. It's not that Rudy replaced Barney—or ever could. It's that Rudy carved out his own special niche in his humans' lives. His crazy wrecking-ball antics and exuberant love demolished their depression and replaced it with joy overflowing.

And despite his talent for being a master of disaster, Rudy has a few boxer nanny genes of his own. He watched over a pair of bunnies his family had and tried to herd them away from the fence where they once found a hole and got out. And when Nicole's now-teenage daughters dive into their pool, he is right there to keep an eye on them. If they don't surface fast enough to suit him, he woofs his concern.

I'm not sure what Nicole and her family believe about God. But she does feel an influence other than human was involved in bringing Rudy to them. There was something about how that initial no turned into a yes. And she's intrigued that both she and her husband have birthdays on the twenty-eighth of a month, and Rudy does too.

As for me, I think Rudy's story is a marvelous illustration of how God sometimes rescues in ways that might at first seem like wreckage. A great Old Testament example is the story of Joseph. He was his father's favorite, so much so that Jacob had a special many-colored robe made for him. This got his 12 older brothers quite jealous. To make matters even worse, Joseph had not one but two dreams that suggested he might rule over his family one day—and was foolish enough to share them.

Joseph's brothers wanted to kill him. Their Plan A was to throw his body into a cistern and say he'd been slain by a wild beast. Only the eldest, Reuben, disagreed. He urged the others not to kill Joseph, and they wound up throwing him into the cistern alive. Reuben's secret intention was to go back alone and rescue Joseph from that pit. But he never got the chance. An Ishmaelite caravan passed by, and the others quickly hatched a Plan B and sold Joseph into slavery for 20 silver shekels.

Reuben was distraught when he learned of this—but not nearly as distraught as Jacob when they showed him Joseph's robe that they had dipped in an animal's blood. Jacob drew the conclusion they desired—his son had been a wild animal's dinner. Jacob was left with a huge, Joseph-shaped hole in his heart. He refused to be comforted by anyone or anything.

Joseph's older brothers were the masters of disaster. It seemed they had wrecked Joseph's life and their father's too. But Someone else was at work. God had a Plan C to use their wreckage for the ultimate rescue of His people. Joseph was sold into slavery in Egypt. Many years and ups and downs later, he interpreted two dreams for Pharaoh. He explained to Pharaoh that they were a warning from God. Egypt would have seven fat years followed by seven lean years of famine. Pharaoh made Joseph the number two man in Egypt and tasked him with storing food so the country was ready for the disaster to come.

Things happened just as Joseph predicted. But that famine didn't hit Egypt only. Jacob and his family were running out of food too, and he sent his sons to Egypt to buy provisions. Joseph realized who they were, but they did not recognize him. He tested them a bit to see if they had changed. When he saw they had, he revealed his true identity. They were petrified, but he told them, "And now, do not be distressed and do not be angry with yourselves for selling me here, because it was to save lives that God sent me ahead of you…God sent me ahead of you to preserve for you a remnant on earth and to save your lives by a great deliverance" (Genesis 45:5,7).

At Joseph's bidding, his whole family joined him in Egypt. Wreckage turned into rescue—they survived the famine. And many long centuries afterward, God chose this people, the Israelites, to birth Jesus the Messiah. When He died on a Roman cross, His disciples thought His death was the ultimate wreckage. But it was the ultimate rescue instead. He defeated sin and death and was raised from the dead, that all who trust in Him might be saved to be with Him forever.

Rudy the canine wrecking ball might not fit the standard job description of a rescuer. But he healed his humans' hearts, and I believe God's hand was in it. Joseph's jealous brothers intended wreckage, but God brought rescue from it, not just for their family but ultimately for all mankind.

Is there wreckage in your life? Don't lose hope. God rescues us in unexpected ways. If, like Joseph, you trust and obey Him and seek His wisdom, who knows how He may turn wreckage into rescue and resurrection for you?

And God spoke to Israel in a vision at night and said, "Jacob! Jacob!"

"Here I am," he replied.

"I am God, the God of your father," he said. "Do not be afraid to go down to Egypt, for I will make you into a great nation there. I will go down to Egypt with you, and I will surely bring you back again. And Joseph's own hand will close your eyes" (Genesis 46:2-4).

CONSIDER THIS:

Has God ever turned wreckage into rescue in your life? What happened? What about it surprised you? What did you learn about yourself? About God?

Why a Dog Goes to a Funeral
God Rescues Our Hearts

The dew of compassion is a tear.
LORD BYRON

God has His ways to comfort us when our hearts are heavy from losing a loved one. Sometimes He even sends a dog to a funeral. That's what He did for my dear friend Lauren, though He had to part the waters of some airline rules to do it.

Lauren was an only child and very close to both her parents. She also loved dogs and had rescued several. One of her beloved pets was a six-pound Chihuahua named Little Man.

Lauren had grown up in Mississippi but was living in California when her mom was diagnosed with cancer. Lauren's mom sought treatment at a cancer center near her daughter. When she died unexpectedly, Lauren and her dad had to fly her mom's body back to Mississippi for burial.

Lauren was single at the time, and her dogs were her kids. She'd planned to leave all of them in the care of dog sitters. But at the last minute, she decided she needed at least one four-pawed pal with her to comfort her shredded heart. She chose Little.

Lauren didn't have a reservation for Little. She didn't have a carrier for him that was airline-approved. She packed him up in his leopard carry bag anyway. As they were boarding the plane, a flight attendant called a halt. This dog wasn't registered to fly and his carrier didn't pass muster. The attendant reluctantly declared the dog grounded.

God decided otherwise. Lauren explained through her tears why she needed Little to go with her. The Lord moved the man's heart. He let Lauren take her dog after all, and just urged her to keep him out of sight. Little landed safely in Mississippi where he played a big role as a four-pawed angel of God's mercy.

"Little went with me everywhere that week as we prepared to send Mom off with banners waving to glory," Lauren recalls. "He went to the visitation, the funeral, and even the graveside. He calmed my heart and made Mom seem not so far away."

A special golden retriever named Titus did something similar for three young boys. They had also lost their mom to cancer, but before they did, they met Titus and his human, Kris, through the Reading Education Assistance Dogs (R.E.A.D.) program. The idea of this program is to help kids relax and read better by letting them read to a loving, nonjudgmental dog. Trained dog/handler teams do this at various locations, including libraries and schools.

These boys developed a bond with Titus, and their mom found out. Kris and Titus were also trained in grief counseling. The mom knew she was dying, and she asked if Titus could come to her funeral and be there for her sons. Kris agreed to bring him.

Titus held the boys' hearts in his paws at both the visitation and the funeral and helped their friends out too. The boys introduced Titus to each person at the visitation. The youngest brother gave out stickers with the dog's name and picture. In the kids' room, Kris let Titus play ball with the boys and their friends. The children brushed him and decorated him with clips. These activities helped them deal with their feelings.

The next day, the boys were all over Titus when he and Kris arrived at the funeral. During the service, Kris parked him in an aisle where the boys could see him. They kept looking over at him, and the youngest got up briefly to pet him. Graveside, the dog lay behind the boys' chairs, and they kept reaching back to touch him. Titus couldn't save them from their tunnel of grief, but his presence was a light in that tunnel that made some very tough days a bit easier to bear.

Two thousand years ago a loving Son who knew He was about to die needed someone to comfort His grieving mother. Jesus's beloved disciple, John, stood with Mary as Jesus hung on the cross and granted His dying request to be like a son to her. He doubtless was a great comfort to her. But her ultimate comfort came when Jesus conquered sin and death and rose from the dead, as all God's children will someday.

God sent Little Man, Titus, and John to give earthly comfort at a time of loss. He sent Jesus to give us heavenly hope. He is the Light at the end of death's tunnel for all who believe, lighting the way to eternal life in Him.

"I am the resurrection and the life. The one who believes in me will live, even though they die; and whoever lives by believing in me will never die. Do you believe this?" (John 11:25-26).

CONSIDER THIS:

When was the last time you lost a loved one? Who or what comforted you most? What is your ultimate hope at the end of death's tunnel?

A Dog-Shaped Anchor
God Keeps Us Grounded

Cast your cares on God; that anchor holds.
FRANK MOORE COLBY OR ALFRED, LORD TENNYSON

Hemingway the pug doesn't look like an anchor, but that's exactly what he has been for his beloved human, Virginia. He has helped to ground her when the seas of life got choppy and might even be the reason she's still afloat.

Virginia is bipolar. She has experienced manic episodes where her brain refused to shut off. These left her exhausted and struggling to focus. She has also swung to the opposite end of the spectrum—too depressed to get out of bed. Virginia told me routines and structure help to keep her stable.

Just having Hemingway to care for has helped anchor Virginia. There have been times when she thought of harming herself, but she didn't. Even though life didn't seem worth living at such moments, she couldn't bear to leave Hemingway or break his heart.

Hemingway senses when Virginia is sick or down and stays close by her side. That's what he did when she was in an abusive relationship. Virginia was lying on the floor beaten, and Hemingway lay right next to her until help arrived. Hemingway also stuck close to Virginia all through her healing process and recovery.

Hemmy is the devoted four-pawed pal who will never leave or forsake Virginia. He follows her into every room of her home. When she sits Indian-style, he comes and leans into her or crawls into her lap. He also loves to lie in her arms like a baby. At night, he stretches out with her in bed and chews on a bone while she reads. Then he curls up under the covers next to her.

Hemmy has also been an anchor for other close loved ones in Virginia's life—both two- and four-footed. After her abusive relationship ended, Virginia went to stay with her friend SJ. Hemmy became pals with SJ's aging Labrador, Hendrix, and SJ thinks Hemmy's presence may have helped Hendrix make it to the ripe old age of 17. But finally it was his time. SJ brought Hemmy along when she took Hendrix to the vet. Virginia met them there. The women lay down beside the big Lab, and Hemmy came and nuzzled his doggie friend's face. After seeing Hendrix off, Hemmy looked after Hendrix's feline soul mate, Lenie Kitty, and became like a brother to this very special cat.

Hemingway has been a faithful, loving anchor in not just the good times but the worst times. God has done the same for His children. Psalm 36:5,7 says,

> Your love, LORD, reaches to the heavens,
>   your faithfulness to the skies…
> How priceless is your unfailing love, O God!

An Old Testament prophet named Jonah experienced God's faithful anchoring at a time when he least deserved it. God had told him to preach repentance to the pagan city of Nineveh. Jonah had a spiritual manic episode and fled in the opposite direction, jumping on a ship for Tarshish. But he had an anchor, God, who wouldn't let him drift too far. God sent a storm that threatened to capsize the boat, and Jonah told the sailors to pitch him overboard. That could have been the end of the story. Seemingly Jonah had no way out. But though he'd rebelled against God, God had not given up on him. He sent a big fish to swallow Jonah and save his life.

After digesting all that had happened for three days in the fish's belly, Jonah came around—sort of. God made the fish vomit Jonah up, and

Jonah preached to Nineveh after all, though grudgingly. The Ninevites repented in dramatic fashion. Seeing this, God spared the city. That should have buoyed Jonah's spirits, but he sank into a deep depression instead. God was his anchor in the midst of that too and tried to do some spiritual attitude adjustment on the prophet with the help of a gourd. How well it worked, the Bible doesn't say.

Hemingway the dog stuck by his precious Virginia regardless of her circumstances. But no dog can be a permanent anchor. Dogs are finite. God and His promises are eternal. Have you put your hope in the anchor that will not fail?

We have this hope as an anchor for the soul, firm and secure. It enters the inner sanctuary behind the curtain, where our forerunner, Jesus, has entered on our behalf. He has become a high priest forever, in the order of Melchizedek (Hebrews 6:19-20).

CONSIDER THIS:

When was the last time God anchored you during one of life's storms? What threatened to set you adrift? How did God stabilize you? Who or what did He use in that process? How might He want you to help anchor someone else?

Four Paws Forward
God Helps Us Go On

Death leaves a heartache no one can heal,
love leaves a memory no one can steal.
HEADSTONE IN IRELAND

Patty got married in her midthirties. Her husband, Steve, was her best friend and soul mate and the love of her life. But in time, she had to share him with another adoring admirer. They got a dog, a basenji they named Murray. And though Murray liked Patty too, Steve was his main man. Over the years, more basenjis were added, but Steve and Murray shared a special bond.

Time passed. Steve turned 53, and despite having diabetes, he seemed in reasonably good health. Then late on the night of Patty's birthday, Steve felt as though he was about to have a heart attack. Patty called the paramedics. They rushed him into an ambulance, but tragedy struck on the way to the hospital. He had the heart attack and slipped into a coma.

Steve's brain swelled. The doctors did tests and told Patty he was brain dead. She didn't want to believe it. She didn't want to give up hope. Not yet. Still, what if it was true? She knew that of all their dogs, Murray would feel Steve's loss the most. Shouldn't she try to give him some closure, just in case?

Dogs were not allowed in the ICU where Steve was. Patty snuck Murray into the hospital through a side door at 3:00 a.m. She hid her 35-pound canine under a baby blanket and carried him past the darkened nurses' station into Steve's room.

Patty figured Murray would beeline for Steve the moment he got the chance. To her shock, he did the opposite. When she removed the blanket and put him down, he made for the door. He wanted nothing to do with the figure on the bed. It was as if Steve wasn't even there.

Which made Patty realize, *Maybe he isn't!*

In those moments, in that room, Murray rescued Patty from false hope. She had thought to give Murray closure, but he did that for her instead. His sense that his master was gone, that only an empty shell of a body remained, helped Patty come to terms with the truth. She still couldn't bring herself to turn off life support, but Steve died the following evening anyway. Patty believes it was less of a shock than it might have been had Murray not set the stage.

Patty credits another basenji, Luna, with nudging her to heal and move forward with her life. Luna was a gift to her from Steve, who wanted another round of pups.

Luna had been a pet shop puppy, but had stayed in the store too long. She didn't quite know what it meant to be a dog. She came to live with Patty and Steve shortly before his death. Their other pups tried to help her become a part of the pack, but she just wasn't getting it. After a number of months, Patty realized the situation wasn't going to work out. Meantime, Luna had had a litter, and Patty kept two offspring, Groovy and Coco Chanel. But she felt Luna would do better somewhere else.

A lovely family with three young boys lived nearby. Patty met them while hiking with Luna, and they fell in love with the dog. After vetting the family to make sure it would be a good fit, she decided to give Luna to them.

When the handoff happened, Patty thought Luna might resist. Luna never even looked back. She leaped joyfully into her bright new future. Patty took a cue from the dog. As much as she missed Steve, and always would, maybe she needed to embrace her future too. Luna's courage gave her courage to go bravely forward into whatever might come next in her life.

Patty and I are casual friends. I don't know all her views on God and spiritual matters, but I think we would both agree that God is at work in people's lives and He uses our pets as one way to speak to our hearts. He used Murray, and then Luna, to help Patty through a heart-wrenching transition and to give her hope.

He used a Moabite woman named Ruth to do the same for a bereft and embittered Hebrew widow named Naomi.

Naomi was married to Elimelech, of the tribe of Judah. They lived in Bethlehem and had two sons. During a time of famine in Israel, Elimelech took his family to live among pagans in Moab. Sadly, he died there. About ten years later, his sons died too, leaving behind their two Moabite widows.

Naomi was crushed. Her loss was terrible on an emotional level, but there was more. In the ancient world, women didn't have the rights that men did. They needed fathers, husbands, or sons to watch over them. Though her Moabite daughters-in-law, Ruth and Orpah, loved her and stayed with her, Naomi felt beaten up by God. How could He allow this to happen? Instead of grieving and then moving forward, she clung to her bitterness.

Then she heard that the famine in Israel was over. She decided to return to her homeland. Orpah and Ruth wanted to come, but she discouraged them. She urged them to go back to their birth families and get new husbands to take care of them.

After an initial refusal, Orpah gave in. Ruth did not. She insisted on staying with Naomi, embracing the God of Israel and remaining loyal till death.

Naomi let Ruth come along after all. But she was still struggling spiritually. When they arrived in Bethlehem, she told the folks who welcomed her back not to call her Naomi, which means "pleasant." "Instead, call me Mara [which means 'bitter'], for the Almighty has made life very bitter for me. I went away full, but the LORD has brought me home empty. Why call me Naomi when the LORD has caused me to suffer and the Almighty has sent such tragedy upon me?" (Ruth 1:20-21 NLT).

Naomi seems to have despaired of things turning around. But God is merciful beyond our comprehension. He knew He would use Ruth to rescue her. They had arrived at harvest time, and Hebrew law allowed the poor to walk behind the harvesters and gather the grain that was dropped. Ruth decided to do this to provide food for herself and Naomi. She chose a field belonging to a wealthy and prominent citizen of Bethlehem named Boaz. Unbeknownst to her, Boaz was Naomi's close relative. He'd heard how much Ruth had done for Naomi, gave her a safe place to work, and showed her great favor as well.

This was just the beginning of God's blessing. There was a legal way for a widow to be provided for. Her closest male relative could buy her husband's land and marry her. The first son from such a union would continue the deceased husband's family name and inherit the land in due time. The relative who did this was called a kinsman redeemer.

Naomi advised Ruth to ask Boaz to be her kinsman redeemer and told her just how to go about it. Boaz took Ruth as his wife. God gave them a son named Obed, and Naomi's family fortunes—and her faith—were restored.

But the rescue doesn't end there. Obed's grandson was a shepherd boy named David who became Israel's greatest king. And from David's line came Jesus, God's Son, the Messiah and ultimate Kinsman Redeemer, who died on a cross to conquer death and save us from our sins. Through faith in Him, we are redeemed to spend eternity as God's children and receive a glorious spiritual inheritance that is ours to enjoy forever.

We live in a fallen world. Loss is part of life. Healthy grieving is a good and necessary thing. But there is a kind of clinging to the past that can embitter us and hinder us from opening our hearts to God's future blessings. God used a pair of dogs to nudge Patty, and He is using her current dog family to help her get healthier physically and mentally.

He used Ruth to heal Naomi's spirit. He knows just what you need too if there's something you are struggling to release. Will you let go and embrace His rescue?

Then Jesus made it clear to his disciples that it was now necessary for him to go to Jerusalem, submit to an ordeal of suffering at the hands of the religious leaders, be killed, and then on the third day be raised up alive. Peter took him in hand, protesting, "Impossible, Master! That can never be!"

But Jesus didn't swerve. "Peter, get out of my way. Satan, get lost. You have no idea how God works" (Matthew 16:21-23 MSG).

CONSIDER THIS:

Are you clinging to someone or something that you need to release so God can bless? Why is it so difficult to let go? Has loss made you bitter toward God? Will you ask Him to rescue you as only He can?

Watchdog of Hearts
God Rescues Us from Fear

A cat bitten once by a snake dreads even rope.
Arab Proverb

Beth's husband, Dean, is a writer and director. But it was God who wrote the script when they needed a dog to guard their hearts.

It all began with a gig that took Dean away from home for several weeks. In fall of 2010, he was working on a TV show in Canada. Beth and their daughters, Erin and Kate, were planning to join him for Thanksgiving. They had their flight. They had their passports. They couldn't wait to be together again. It was Monday of Thanksgiving week, and it wouldn't be long now…

It would be longer than they thought.

At around noon, Beth unlocked the door of their La Crescenta, California, home and got a huge shock. Their house had been ransacked! Thieves had taken not only valuables, but some of their personal paperwork and their passports too.

No way could those passports be replaced in time. Their family reunion had been stolen. Worse, so had their peace of mind. Home invasion sets a person's mind and heart and nerves on edge. It replaces that warm, safe-at-home feeling with fear and foreboding. Beth took to hiding important papers under couch cushions when the house would be empty. When she brought the girls home from school, they cringed walking through the front door. She would always check the living room, fearing an intruder. And even after Dean returned, his loved ones figured that sooner or later, he would probably have another extended out-of-town job.

Clearly, something had to be done. They could install an alarm system, but Beth wasn't crazy about this option. There was another possibility, though. It had tugged at her even before the break-in. *Maybe their family needed a dog.*

It took a few months for Beth and her family to actually take the dog leap. There were logistics to consider. They were in a coyote area and would have to take appropriate precautions. They also needed to figure out what they would do with a pet when they went on the last-minute family getaways they loved. But in June, they started searching for a rescue dog online. They were drawn to one at the Pasadena shelter. Beth and the girls went for a meet and greet. Things didn't click, but on their way out, daughter Kate spied "this cute white dog."

They inquired about the female Jack Russell terrier/Chihuahua mix. She'd been at the shelter only for five days. Someone had found her wandering near the 110 freeway. She'd come in with road grease on her back, but her spirit was pure gold. She was curious and sweet. She hopped right up onto Kate's lap and grabbed their hearts.

Beth and the girls thought they wanted this dog, but they needed Dad to vet the prospective new family member too. Next day he joined Beth at the shelter at lunchtime. The dog tried to claim his lap too— and claimed his heart in the process. They began the adoption and, four days later, brought the white dog home and named her Pippa.

In the next couple of months, 18-pound Pippa blossomed into a watchdog. Beth told me no one can walk on their street without Pippa sounding off. She barks and runs to the door when anyone is there. If she senses her people are okay with the visitor, she calms down. But if the newcomer is a stranger or her people are ill at ease, she's not happy. She erupts in a nonstop lava flow of barks. In some cases, Beth has had to put her in another room.

Pippa also has protective instincts toward their favorite neighbors. Pippa tries to look out the window at their driveway and keep watch over their home too. These folks have daughters the same age as Beth's girls. They dog-sit Pippa when Beth's family is out of town.

Pippa's barking is a great deterrent, but whether she has ever scared off potential intruders is anybody's guess. What she would do if someone broke in is a guess too. Even when she's been wary of someone, she has never bitten. But she has certainly guarded her family's hearts and eased their fears. Beth doesn't hide papers under the couch cushions anymore. Her nerves don't jangle when her older daughter, now driving, comes home to an empty house. That's because Pippa is there to welcome her and be a four-legged sentry, sounding off if something is amiss. And when Dean returned to Canada for several more weeks this past fall, his family's hearts didn't crumble. They knew Pippa was on watch.

King Hezekiah's heart didn't totally crumble either when he faced the consummate home invasion—an Assyrian army at Jerusalem's gates. That's because he knew that God was there to watch over him and his people.

Hezekiah was an Old Testament king of Judah. Unlike some rulers, he was a godly man. In 2 Kings 18:5-6 we read, "Hezekiah trusted in the LORD, the God of Israel. There was no one like him among all the kings of Judah, either before him or after him. He held fast to the LORD and did not stop following him; he kept the commands the LORD had given Moses."

Hezekiah began his reign at 25 years of age. He cut off tribute payments to Assyria. In the sixth year of his rule, Assyria conquered the northern kingdom, Israel, and took its people into exile. Eight years later, the Assyrians and their king, Sennacherib, moved against Judah. Hezekiah sent tribute, hoping to appease them. No go! The Assyrian forces arrived at Jerusalem's gates. Three of Sennacherib's top commanders had a powwow with three of Hezekiah's head honchos in full hearing of those on the city walls. The Assyrians even spoke Hebrew to be sure the people understood their posturing and were properly terrified of the invaders. Among other things, they said, "Don't listen to

Hezekiah. Don't listen to his lies, telling you 'GOD will save us.' Has there ever been a god anywhere who delivered anyone from the king of Assyria?" (2 Kings 18:32-33 MSG).

Hezekiah appealed to God and sent word to Isaiah the prophet, pleading with him to pray for the remnant of Israel. And God, who not only guards hearts but wields ultimate power over people and nations and all creation, responded. Through Isaiah, He told Hezekiah not to worry. He, God, would handle Sennacherib. Hezekiah took God at His word. When Sennacherib threatened some more, Hezekiah brought those threats to God in prayer.

> But now O GOD, *our* God,
>   save us from raw Assyrian power;
> Make all the kingdoms on earth know
>   that you are GOD, the one and only God.
>   (2 Kings 19:19 MSG)

Once again, Isaiah sent word to the king confirming that God had heard and God would act. Second Kings 19:35-37 (MSG) tells how.

> And it so happened that that very night an angel of GOD came and massacred 185,000 Assyrians. When the people of Jerusalem got up next morning, there it was—a whole camp of corpses!

> Sennacherib king of Assyria got out of there fast, headed straight home for Nineveh, and stayed put. One day when he was worshiping in the temple of his god Nisroch, his sons Adrammelech and Sharezer murdered him and then escaped to the land of Ararat. His son Esarhaddon became the next king.

Pippa guards her humans' home and hearts, but ultimately, God does. Beth and her family love the Lord. They know Pippa is His gift to give them peace of mind. They know, as Hezekiah did, that God is more powerful than any invader or intruder who would do them harm. That includes the army of fears that threatens to invade and attack their hearts—and ours—in this fallen, broken world. Why not pray and call on God to slay them and keep you safe in Him instead?

Don't worry about anything; instead, pray about everything. Tell God what you need, and thank him for all he has done. Then you will experience God's peace, which exceeds anything we can understand. His peace will guard your hearts and minds as you live in Christ Jesus (Philippians 4:6-7 NLT).

CONSIDER THIS:

Are fears and anxieties trying to invade your heart right now? How is that affecting your life? How is it influencing your relationship with God? Have you asked God to slay your fears and guard your heart? What promises from Scripture might help you trust Him to do so?

A Dog, a Boy, and a Puzzle
God's Rescue Is a Journey

*To get through the hardest journey we need take only
one step at a time, but we must keep on stepping.*
CHINESE PROVERB

Joshua the boy was already on a journey when he met Journey the dog. He had autism and cerebral palsy. Until age four, he couldn't speak words. But he had a loving, involved family and was given intensive therapy. By age seven, he had made huge strides. A casual observer might have thought he was a typical young boy.

Ginger, Joshua's mom, knew otherwise. Though her son had come so far, something was still lacking. Josh wasn't making normal emotional connections. When it came to loving his siblings and parents deeply or having empathy for their feelings, he just didn't seem quite able to do it. And though he was never unkind to the family cat and dog, he was also a bit indifferent to them. If his emotional life was a puzzle, it seemed as though a piece was missing, and Ginger wasn't sure her son would ever find it.

Then Josh's therapist started taking him to a local library once a month to read to a dog. That dog, Journey, and his person, Mary, were part of the Reading Education Assistance Dogs (R.E.A.D.) program.

Journey's path to involvement in R.E.A.D. had had a few speed bumps of its own. This gorgeous golden retriever had been a handful as a pup. He became a champion show dog but was rather full of himself. He didn't care much for obedience training. Mary decided he needed a job. She tried him in tracking, but it didn't work out—he preferred eating grass to finding things. But he loved people and going to new places. So, when Journey reached age five or six and had calmed down a bit, Mary decided to get him certified as a therapy dog. He flunked his first evaluation when he refused to "down." But he passed with flying colors six months later. After working in local nursing homes and as a demo dog in school safety programs, he jumped in with all four paws as a R.E.A.D. dog. Once a month, he showed up at a local library and listened as kids read to him and Mary gave them positive reinforcement.

That's when Journey's and Josh's paths crossed. At first, Mary didn't know that Josh was autistic. She did notice that he wouldn't sit still for long. He would read half a page and then announce, "I'm done." Still, he loved his time with Journey and wouldn't read with any other pup.

As Mary got to know Josh's family, she learned more about the boy's background. And as Josh kept reading to Journey, his own journey changed. He started loving on his own dog and cat. He began to notice and ask about how others in his family were feeling. He grew in empathy and caring. Thanks to a loving, patient therapy dog, a door was unlocked in this young boy's life. A puzzle piece fell into place. A child's emotional life was made more whole.

But that is not *quite* the end of this journey.

After Josh and Journey had been reading together for many months, Journey was diagnosed with cancer. It was not operable or treatable. This took place a little before Thanksgiving of 2010, and Journey went to the R.E.A.D. program only one more time. After that, he was too ill.

Mary thought about Josh and how attached he was to the dog. She realized he might need closure. She called Ginger and told her what was happening. Journey was too weak to leave the house, but Mary said Josh could come to visit and read to him one last time. That is, unless Ginger felt it might be too much for her son to handle.

Ginger said she'd give it some thought. She called Mary back the next day. "I spoke with Josh, and he wants to say good-bye," she said.

Journey was lying on the sofa on the appointed day. He perked up when his buddy walked in. Mary had laid out some books for Josh to choose from, but he didn't like any of them. Mary told him he could pick one from her bookshelves instead.

Josh searched the shelves and chose a book about a dog chapel where people can celebrate their dogs and honor those who have passed on. Of all the books in that room, Josh picked this one. Reading it aloud provided an opportunity to talk about Journey's dying without being specific.

In the book there's a dog with angel wings. Josh said, "Journey will have wings too." Josh started petting Journey's head and told his four-legged pal, "I'll see you in heaven."

At one point Josh's mom was just sobbing. Ever the sweet, empathetic pup, Journey laid his head in her lap.

When she's not working with her therapy dogs, Mary trains other people's canines. Sometime after Journey died on January 11, 2011, Josh's family got a new puppy. Ginger took the dog to Mary's puppy class, and Josh came with her one night. He told Mary, "I miss Journey." Mary said, "I do too." Mary has another R.E.A.D. dog, Miles, and Josh has read to him a couple of times now. Though Journey's time on earth is over, Josh's journey continues.

When I think of Josh and Journey and their story, it reminds me of how God works with us. So much of God's rescue is a process. And there are always puzzle pieces God has that we don't. This was certainly the case with an Old Testament patriarch named Abraham. He was told to leave his family and his homeland and go to a place he knew nothing about—just because God said so. If he obeyed, God promised to make him the father of a great nation and bless all the peoples of the earth through him.

Abraham did as God asked, even though he didn't have all the puzzle pieces. He especially didn't know how he could found a nation when he and his wife Sarah were past childbearing age. But in time,

Sarah bore a son. They named him Isaac. And it seemed God's promise would come true.

Then, God threw Abraham a curve. He ordered Abraham to take his son to a land called Moriah and sacrifice the boy on a mountain. How could God's promise possibly come true if he did that?

Abraham didn't have the missing puzzle piece. But he had faith in God. He took the journey with Isaac and climbed the mountain. He laid his beloved son on the altar. And at the last second, God stayed his hand and provided a ram instead—a ram who foreshadowed the Messiah, the Lamb of God, the Son of God, who would come to earth in human form, live a sinless life, and die on Calvary as a sacrifice for the sins of all mankind.

Just as Journey helped make Josh whole by loving him and unlocking his heart, God makes His children whole by His redemptive love. It is a process and it is ongoing in this life. But one day our earthly journey will end, the last puzzle pieces will slip into place, and we will dwell in God's presence forever!

Dear friends, now we are children of God, and what we will be has not yet been made known. But we know that when Christ appears, we shall be like him, for we shall see him as he is (1 John 3:2).

CONSIDER THIS:

Has God ever given you a missing puzzle piece that healed or rescued you? What was it? What was your journey with God to receive it? How might God use your love and patience to provide a healing puzzle piece for someone else?

Meet the Author

M.R. Wells has coauthored five devotional books for pet lovers. She has also written extensively for children's television and video programming, including several Disney shows, the animated PBS series *Adventures from the Book of Virtues*, and the action video series *Bibleman*. She shares her Southern California home with the puppies and kitties she adores: Becca, Marley, Mica, Muffin, Bo, and Bonbon.

For more information visit
www.fourpawsfromheaven.com

Great Dog Stories
*Inspiration and Humor from Our Canine
Companions*

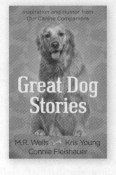

From the authors of *Four Paws from Heaven* comes
a new collection of devotional tales. In these heartwarming stories, the authors share wisdom gleaned
from years of training, guiding, and loving the
canines in their lives. Readers will discover powerful
spiritual insights, including:

- the blessing of true
  companionship
- the gift of unconditional love
- the joy of adoption
- the power of obedience
- the comfort of resting in the
  Master's arms

Everyone who has loved a dog will find encouragement and hope in
these touching stories—reminders that these faithful, devoted companions
are part of God's great plan for their lives.

Four Paws from Heaven
Devotions for Dog Lovers

With over 100,000 copies sold, *Four Paws from
Heaven* is a surefire hit! Now with a fun new cover,
three talented writers and dog masters share wisdom
gleaned while walking through life alongside four
paws. Through dog tales and human stories, this pack
of short, enjoyable devotions focuses on spiritual lessons, including:

- who we are on the inside
  matters
- rebellion blocks blessings
- boundaries are for our own
  good
- using our talents glorifies
  God
- if we always bark, we won't
  hear instructions

Pet lovers will find encouragement and guidance for their own life
through invitations to reflect on the love, companionship, and insight dogs
give to those who love them.

Paws for Reflection
Devotions for Dog Lovers

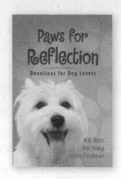

The great writing team behind the popular *Four Paws from Heaven* presents even more reasons for readers to celebrate dogs and faith. This gathering of pup tales combines true stories about dogs with what we can learn from them for handling real-life situations. More than 50 new, humorous, poignant, and spiritually insightful stories are packed together under themed sections:

- Paws for Love: Curl Up with the Master
- Paws for Training: Sit, Stay, Grow
- Paws for Healing: Let God Smooth Out the Tangles
- Paws for Guidance: Follow Your Alpha

This special gathering of short devotions reminds readers about the wonderful treats of love, faithfulness, and companionship.

To learn more about Harvest House books and
to read sample chapters, visit our website:

www.harvesthousepublishers.com

HARVEST HOUSE PUBLISHERS
EUGENE, OREGON

*What dogs
can teach us
about life, love, and loyalty*

From a coauthor of *Four Paws from Heaven* (nearly 125,000 copies sold) comes a new devotional for everyone who's ever loved a dog. This collection of short, inspirational stories features service dogs, therapy dogs... ...ve helped their humans in sometimes unex...

- 🐾 what dogs can teach us about the care and faithfulness of the Master
- 🐾 the blessings of unconditional love and true loyalty
- 🐾 the unusual means God sometimes uses to come to our aid
- 🐾 how helping a friend can help us too
- 🐾 what we can learn from dogs about facing life's challenges

These heartwarming tales of dog heroics will teach you that who you are on the inside matters most—and that with God (and a furry friend) on your side, there's no obstacle you can't overcome.

M.R. Wells has written extensively for children's television and video programming, including several Disney shows, the animated PBS series *Adventures from The Book of Virtues*, and the action video series *Bibleman*. She lives in California with three dogs and three cats.

Devotional
ISBN 978-0-7369-4956-9

**HARVEST HOUSE
PUBLISHERS**
® EUGENE, OREGON 97402
HarvestHousePublishers.com

U.S. $12.99